HEINRICH VON KLEIST'S DRAMAS

MODERN LANGUAGE STUDIES

MODERN LANGUAGE STUDIES

HEINRICH von KLEIST'S DRAMAS

E. L. STAHL

TAYLOR PROFESSOR OF THE GERMAN LANGUAGE
AND LITERATURE IN THE UNIVERSITY OF OXFORD
FELLOW OF THE QUEEN'S COLLEGE
STUDENT EMERITUS OF CHRIST CHURCH

BASIL BLACKWELL
OXFORD
1961

TO THE MEMORY OF
MY MOTHER

© *Basil Blackwell, 1961*

PRINTED IN GREAT BRITAIN
BY THE COMPTON PRINTING WORKS (LONDON) LTD., LONDON, N.1
FOR BASIL BLACKWELL & MOTT LTD.
AND BOUND BY
THE KEMP HALL BINDERY, OXFORD·

PREFACE

MY principal aim in writing this short book on the dramas of Heinrich von Kleist was to give a general rather than a detailed account. I have purposely omitted to discuss aspects of his work which have received particular attention in the best known books on the subject. My discussion of one or two of the plays has therefore been necessarily brief. The edition of Kleist's works from which I quote is that by Erich Schmidt, Georg Minde-Pouet and Reinhold Steig in *Meyers Klassiker Ausgaben*. References to the text of this edition will be found at the end of my translation of each of the passages quoted.

My grateful thanks are due to the Publishers and the Editors of *Modern Language Studies*, particularly to Professor James Boyd, and to my colleagues Mr. J. Knight Bostock and Mr. H. G. Barnes, all of whom greatly assisted me with their valuable suggestions. I also wish to express my thanks to the Curators of the Taylor Institution for their generous grant from the Gerrans Fund towards the cost of publication. To my wife I must, however inadequately, express my gratitude for her constant encouragement and help.

E. L. S.

Oxford.
August 1948

PREFACE TO REVISED EDITION

IN this photolithographic reprint I have not been able to make radical changes. It has, however, been possible for me to adopt some of the many excellent suggestions made by Professors W. Silz and John T. Krumpelmann. For the earlier volume, which was written at the end of the war, I had to rely on the 1904 edition of Kleist's works by Erich Schmidt, Minde-Pouet and Steig. The improved 1937 edition was not available to me at that time. For the present reprint I have made some alterations based on this edition, but all textual references are still to the 1904 edition. To a large extent the bibliography, which does not claim to be complete, has been brought up to date.

E. L. S.

Oxford.
November 1960

CONTENTS

HEINRICH VON KLEIST'S DRAMAS

INTRODUCTION

I

AMONG the pessimistic writers of the nineteenth century in Germany there were some who based their views on the conviction that the weakness of human nature was the root of man's unhappiness, while others believed that the fault lay with a malevolent external power which rules the world. Much of the uncertainty and the disorientation so manifest in the spiritual life of Germany in that century is reflected in the exclusive emphasis that was laid on one side of the problem or the other, upon the innate frailty of human nature on the one hand, and upon the evil power outside on the other hand.

In the field of the German drama this difference is shown in the work of Grillparzer and of Kleist. The ultimate source of Kleist's pessimism was his inability to believe in a benevolent Deity, while Grillparzer's pessimism was inspired by a profound distrust of human nature. If by the term 'Fate tragedy' is meant a drama in which the sufferings of the characters may be traced solely to the workings of a power beyond the control of man, then Grillparzer was justified in asserting that even *Die Ahnfrau* is not a drama of this type. He believed that life was tragic mainly because men were led astray by their own desires and ambitions and because they strove to exceed the limits set for them by an inscrutable, but by no means malevolent, Providence. In his dramas human beings are the agents responsible for their own misfortunes.

Against the inauguration of a 'Schicksalstragödie' Lessing protested in vain.[1] For him the doctrine that in tragedy suffering should be caused by a flaw of character was the essential corollary of a belief in a wise and benevolent Providence and of a conviction that dramatists should not sow the seeds of doubt in the mind of the spectator regarding the nature of the Universe. For him, the optimist, as for

---

[1] Cf. esp. *Hamburgische Dramaturgie*, 'Stück' 79.

Grillparzer, the pessimist, tragedy should represent events not possessing a metaphysical significance.

Even Lessing's authority was unable to prevent the growth of a state of mind in Germany which made the drama the vehicle for pessimistic reflections on the ultimate meaning of life, and Heinrich von Kleist became, in this respect, the greatest antipode of Lessing. Neither in Goethe and Schiller, nor in the minor writers of the 'Sturm und Drang' is the fundamental pessimism to be found, which is the source of Kleist's first dramatic productions. Faust, it is true, laments the limitations of human nature, the inability of man to know 'was die Welt im Innersten zusammenhält'. But *Faust* was not conceived as a tragedy of the impotence of the human mind and indeed in Faust's recognition 'dem Tüchtigen ist die Welt nicht stumm' and in the divine sanction granted to his striving, in the divine forgiveness even of his sins, lies the guarantee of his salvation.

Kleist eventually arrived at a similar affirmation of effort in the world, but only after he had been driven to the limits of negation and distrust. Indeed, his affirmation of life in *Prinz Friedrich von Homburg* does not answer the religious doubts which he had expressed in *Die Familie Schroffenstein* and in *Amphitryon*, in the sense in which Faust's salvation answers the problems raised at the beginning of Goethe's drama. Kleist was able to give a positive valuation to life only because he shelved his metaphysical questionings, not because he solved them. An explanation of this apparently unmotivated change of attitude may be sought in Kleist's emotional and intellectual experiences.

There are many events in Kleist's life where lack of evidence prevents us from gaining a true estimate of his development as a poet. His journey to Würzburg in 1800, his visit to Paris in 1801, his life in Königsberg, Dresden and Berlin from 1805 to 1811 represent the crucial periods in his literary career, but we do not possess sufficient data to explain the rapid growth of his art and the sudden changes in his mental outlook. He lived in comparative obscurity and there is no coherent record from his friends or from his letters to assist us in viewing his dramas in perspective. The dramas themselves offer the most reliable testimony of his development and while this circumstance has enabled critics to concentrate on the substance and the aesthetic form of his works, it has also led to the most divergent interpretations of their essential meaning.

However, the importance of at least three major intellectual influences on Kleist's life and work has been generally recognized. They are: first, his assimilation of pre-Kantian philosophy; secondly, the impact of Kant or the followers of Kant on his thought; and thirdly, his interest in the ideas of G. H. von Schubert and of Adam Müller. Although it is not possible to establish complete agreement about the precise effect of these intellectual experiences on Kleist's work, and although we may never know to what extent these experiences determined his psychological and artistic development or were determined by it, the influence of Kant, Schubert and Müller appear to be the most clearly recognizable milestones indicating his spiritual progress from pessimism to a guarded optimism.

Of another order, but equally significant, is the effect of the Napoleonic Wars on Kleist's mind and art. Their importance lies in the fact that they took the place of the earlier intellectual influences and that, to a large extent, they effaced these earlier experiences. They closed an important chapter in Kleist's life and opened a new one. The Napoleonic Wars turned his mind from his previous pre-occupation with the metaphysical conditions of existence and directed it towards the acceptance of practical values, and they impelled him to portray characters who represented social and national causes and conflicts. In the dramas from *Robert Guiskard* to *Käthchen von Heilbronn* Kleist's characters are engaged in conflicts whose source is the metaphysical condition of man, in *Die Hermannsschlacht* and in *Prinz Friedrich von Homburg* they contend for values that belong to the concrete life of nations and of society. For the earlier plays it is the absolute, for the later plays it is the positive mode of human existence in which the characters have their origin and their being.

This change of dramatic purpose, far-reaching though it was, did not radically alter the nature of Kleist's dramatic art. The under-lying unity of his work is revealed in his persistent treatment of the themes of error and deceit. They occur in his earlier no less than in his later dramas, in his tragic as well as his non-tragic plays, and similarly in almost the whole body of his prose tales. The dominating position which these themes occupy in the entire work of Kleist gives them a peculiar significance. Their meaning is revealed at the outset of his literary career and they supply us with a key to the under-standing of his artistic development.

2

The impetus to write dramas originated in Kleist's life when his youthful reflections suffered the impact of Kant's philosophy. As a young man he had adopted the optimistic views that were current in Germany in the eighteenth century. Deriving from Leibniz, they had been combined with the eudemonist principles of Shaftesbury's system in the popular philosophy of Wolff and Garve. Upon this system Kleist based his early belief in divine benevolence and the view that human beings were destined to achieve happiness on earth. He expressed these ideas in his *Aufsatz, den sicheren Weg des Glücks zu finden* (1799): 'Irgendwo in der Schöpfung muss es sich gründen, der Inbegriff aller Dinge muss die Ursachen und die Bestandteile des Glückes enthalten, mein Freund, denn die Gottheit wird die Sehnsucht nach Glück nicht täuschen, die sie selbst unauslöschlich in unserer Seele erweckt hat.' [i]. Kleist's arguments in support of this view were even less convincing than those of Garve, for he lacked the profounder intuitions upon which Lessing had based his belief in Providence.

But eudemonism is not the only principle to be found in Kleist's early writings. The later direction of his thought under the influence of Kant's philosophy is already indicated in a letter which he wrote to his sister Ulrike in May 1799. His trust in what he considered to be 'der Inbegriff aller Dinge' inspired in him a resolve to lead his life in accordance with a 'Lebensplan' of his own devising. He firmly believed that man possessed the power to rule his own life, to choose his own happiness, to guide the hand of Fate instead of being guided by it, but while asserting this belief he betrayed a more deep-seated fear:

Tausend Menschen höre ich reden und sehe ich handeln, und es fällt mir nicht ein, nach dem Warum? zu fragen. Sie selbst wissen es nicht, dunkle Neigungen leiten sie, der Augenblick bestimmt ihre Handlungen. Sie bleiben für immer unmündig und ihr Schicksal ein Spiel des Zufalls. Sie fühlen sich wie von unsichtbaren Kräften geleitet und gezogen, sie folgen ihnen im Gefühl ihrer Schwäche wohin es sie auch führt, zum Glücke, das sie dann nur halb geniessen, zum Unglück, das sie dann doppelt fühlen. Eine solche sclavische Hingebung in die Launen des Tyrannen Schicksal, ist nun freilich eines freien, denkenden Menschen höchst unwürdig. Ein freier denkender Mensch bleibt da nicht stehen, wo der Zufall ihn hinstösst; oder wenn er bleibt, so bleibt er aus Gründen, aus Wahl des Bessern. Er fühlt, dass man sich über das Schicksal erheben könne, ja, dass es im richtigen Sinne selbst möglich sei, das Schicksal zu leiten.' 'Ja, es ist mir so unbegreiflich, wie ein Mensch ohne Lebensplan leben könne, und ich fühle, an der Sicherheit, mit welcher ich die Gegenwart benutze, an der Ruhe, mit welcher ich in die Zukunft blicke, so innig, welch' ein unschätzbares Glück mir mein Lebensplan gewährt, und der Zustand, ohne Lebensplan, ohne feste Bestimmung, immer schwankend zwischen unsichern Wünschen, immer ein Widerspruch mit meinen Pflichten, ein Spiel des Zufalls, eine Puppe am Drahte des Schicksals — dieser unwürdige Zustand scheint mir so verächtlich, und würde mich so unglücklich machen, dass mir der Tod bei weitem wünschenswerter wäre. [ii].

Below the surface of Kleist's confident optimism lurked a profound despair, a presentiment of the uncertainty and the instability of life. He clung to the promise of happiness and to the prospect of a rationally ordered life because they were the only guarantees that could offer him security and comfort. In his early letters and in the *Aufsatz* he justified the step he had taken in resigning his commission in the Prussian army by proclaiming the freedom of man to decide his own fate, but these writings testify to his fear of life as much as they reveal his confidence in his own powers. Even at this early stage he was aware of an incalculable force both within and outside him. He dreaded above all to become 'the puppet of Fate', a victim of his own conflicting passions and of the uncontrollable force of chance. The smooth surface of his eudemonism was a façade concealing his profound misgivings and hesitations. Like the letter to Ulrike, Kleist's *Aufsatz, den sicheren Weg des Glücks zu finden* reveals his sense of uncertainty:

Sie hören mich so viel und so lebhaft von der Tugend sprechen, und doch weiss ich, dass Sie mit diesem Worte nur einen dunkeln Sinn verknüpfen, Lieber, es geht mir wie Ihnen, wenn ich gleich so viel davon rede. Es erscheint mir nur wie ein Hohes, Erhabenes, Unnennbares, für das ich vergebens ein Wort suche, um es durch die Sprache, vergebens eine Gestalt, um es durch ein Bild auszudrücken. Und dennoch strebe ich ihm mit der innigsten Innigkeit entgegen als stünde es klar und deutlich vor meiner Seele. Alles was ich davon weiss, ist, dass es die unvollkommenen Vorstellungen, deren ich jetzt nur fähig bin, gewiss auch enthalten wird; aber ich ahnde noch mehr, noch etwas Höheres, noch etwas Erhaberes, und das ist es recht eigentlich, was ich nicht ausdrücken und formen kann. . . . Und nun, mein Freund, will ich Ihnen eine Lehre geben, von deren Wahrheit mein Geist zwar überzeugt ist, obgleich mein Herz ihr unaufhörlich widerspricht. Diese Lehre ist, von den Wegen, die zwischen dem höchsten äussern Glück und Unglück liegen, grade nur auf der Mittelstrasse zu wandern, und unsre Wünsche nie auf die schwindlichen Höhen zu richten. So sehr ich jetzt noch die Mittelstrassen aller Art hasse, weil ein natürlich heftiger Trieb im Innern mich verführt, so ahnde ich dennoch, dass Zeit und Erfahrung mich einst davon überzeugen werden, dass sie dennoch die besten sein. [iii].

This was the authentic voice of Kleist, the Kleist who suffered the conflict between his mind and his heart, who was driven to extremes of joy and sorrow, forsaking the middle path, and who became a poet when he discarded the eudemonist philosophy of his youth and found the words and the images that expressed the secret promptings of his soul. The poet in him was born when the layers of acquired philosophy were removed and the deeper sources of his being were fully uncovered and resolutely acknowledged.

As with the Schiller of *Die Theosophie des Julius* the impact of Kant's philosophical criticism proved overwhelmingly destructive, 'alles zermalmend', and it produced in Kleist, as it had done in Schiller, a radical scepticism. But whereas Schiller set to work to cover up the breach by means of the very discipline that had destroyed his early beliefs, by the assimilation of Kant's ethical and aesthetic principles, Kleist followed his scepticism through to its psychological, not its logical, conclusions. Schiller, the poet, recovered from the shock by suspending his poetic activity in order to emerge a poet reformed, Kleist became a poet because he had suffered this reversal. Philosophy was not the means by which he regained his equilibrium. Indeed, he never achieved a stable attitude to life, although in his years of maturity he desired to affirm its values. His life and work reveals a recurrent series of alternating moods, and neither an intellectual discipline nor a settled activity produced in him that stability of outlook which is characteristic of Schiller's 'classical' creed, the mainspring of his maturest poetic productions.

Even before he fully realized the fallacy of his former beliefs, Kleist was aware of his own instability. This is shown in a passage from the *Aufsatz, den sichern Weg des Glücks zu finden*:

Jetzt freilich wanken wir noch auf regellosen Bahnen umher, aber, mein Freund, das ist uns als Jünglinge zu verzeihen. Die innere Gärung ineinander wirkender Kräfte, die uns in diesem Alter erfüllt, lässt keine Ruhe im Denken und Handeln zu. Wir kennen die Beschwörungsformel noch nicht, die Zeit allein führt sie mit sich, um die wunderbar ungleichartigen Gestalten, die in unserm Innern wühlen und durcheinander treiben, zu besänftigen und zu beruhigen. Und alle Jünglinge, die wir um und neben uns sehen, teilen ja mit uns dieses Schicksal. Alle ihre Schritte und Bewegungen scheinen nur die Wirkung eines unfühlbaren aber gewaltigen Stosses zu sein, der sie unwiderstehlich mit sich fortreisst. Sie erscheinen mir wie Kometen, die in regellosen Kreisen das Weltall durchschweifen, bis sie endlich eine Bahn und ein Gesetz der Bewegung finden. [iv].

As in his letter to Ulrike of May, 1799, Kleist here accounts for his emotional instability by postulating the interference of an external power and he is even more emphatic concerning the irresistible strength of this force. The more he matured, the more he realized that the 'inward fermentation', the 'violent impulse within', were his own essential reality and that from them rather than from a desire to discover a 'magic formula' and 'a settled course' derived his poetic impulses. His restlessness was symptomatic of the malady of a young generation for which Goethe's and Schiller's classical ideals did not represent a real issue. Therefore Kant's philosophy could not supply Kleist with the means of solving the problems which it had raised for him. There could be no progress for him except in accordance with the natural tendencies of his inner self. Philosophy aided him by releasing forces hidden within him, by which he produced poetry, but philosophy did not belong to the fabric of his poetry. He was not a philosophical poet in the sense in which Schiller, to a large extent, was a philosophical poet. Philosophy only set in motion the spiritual activity from which resulted Kleist's poetic creativeness.

It would be an exaggeration to claim that he absorbed, as Schiller endeavoured to do, the essential features of Kant's thought. Although he conceived the plan of settling with Wilhelmine von Zenge in France in order to introduce Kant's philosophy to the French people, his knowledge of this philosophy was perhaps rudimentary. He did not possess Schiller's intellectual powers nor did he become acquainted with the whole of Kant, but only with a portion of his thought.[1] Kleist's view of life resulting from his reading of 'die neuere sogenannte Kantische Philosophie' was by no means truly Kantian. It is important to observe what aspect of Kant's teaching appealed to Kleist and which side of it he failed to assimilate.

The first signs of Kant's influence on his ideas of life are found in his letter to Wilhelmine von Zenge from Würzburg on September 15, 16, 1800:

Über den Zweck unseres ganzen ewigen Daseins nachzudenken, auszuforschen, ob der Genuss der Glückseligkeit (wie Epikur meinte) oder die Erreichung der Vollkommenheit (wie Leibnitz glaubte) oder die Erfüllung der trocknen Pflicht (wie Kant versichert) der letzte Zweck des Menschen sei, das ist selbst für Männer unfruchtbar und oft verderblich . . . Urteile selbst, wie können wir beschränkte Wesen, die wir von der Ewigkeit nur ein so unendlich kleines Stück, unser spannenlanges Erdenleben übersehen, wie können wir uns getrauen, den Plan, den die Natur

---

[1] Many critics, however, believe that he had made a thorough study of Kant and Fichte (cf. E. Cassirer: *H. v. Kleist und die Kantische Philosophie, Idee und Gestalt,* 1921) and that he was influenced by Fichte rather than by Kant. New light has recently been thrown on this subject proving Kleist's indebtedness to Fichte. Cf. D. F. S. Scott, *Mod. Lang. Review,* XLII, pp. 474 ff. Cf. also the convincing new interpretation by L. Muth, *Kleist und Kant,* 1954.

für die Ewigkeit entwarf, zu ergründen? Und wenn dies nicht möglich ist, wie kann irgend eine gerechte Gottheit von uns verlangen, in diesen ihren ewigen Plan einzugreifen, von uns, die wir nicht einmal im Stande sind, ihn zu denken? Aber die Bestimmung unseres irdischen Daseins, die können wir allerdings unzweifelhaft herausfinden, und diese zu erfüllen, das kann daher die Gottheit auch wohl mit Recht von uns fordern. [v].

The first effects of the *Critique of Pure Reason* on Kleist's thought were both negative and positive. He was compelled to abandon his 'Lebensplan' in so far as it had been based on his speculations concerning the ultimate destiny of man. In his *Aufsatz* he had asserted that man could guide the powers that rule his life. Now the fallacy of this belief was brought home to him. He recognized with Kant that metaphysical reflections upon the nature of human existence were idle dreams, and he accepted Kant's conclusion that man should seek to base his life not on abstract principles, but on the concrete task of performing his duty.

The negative aspect of Kant's *Critique*, however, overshadowed its positive side for Kleist. The categorical imperative 'Erfülle deine Pflicht' proved of little value to a man who did not know what his duty was. Kleist's letters from 1800 till 1802 bear ample testimony to the fact that he could not make up his mind what profession he should choose. He considered devoting his life to study, he thought of entering the Prussian civil service, he wanted to buy a farm in Switzerland, but none of these plans matured. His inability to arrive at a decision in his relationship with Wilhelmine von Zenge is another symptom of his perpetual restlessness. This instability was intensified by Kant's destructive criticism of the grounds of his former beliefs and finally resulted in his conversion to a thoroughly pessimistic view of life. His restlessness grew into despair and his uncertainty turned into doubt. Whereas Kant had only examined the basis of human knowledge and proved its limitations, Kleist proceeded to demur against God for having put these limitations upon man, to proclaim the relativity of all knowledge and to assert the worthlessness of life. He was thrown from the extreme of optimism to the extreme of pessimism out of which grew his first dramatic productions.

His letters to Wilhelmine von Zenge, notably those of September 18, 1800, March 22, 1801, July 21, 1801, and August 15, 1801, are the only documents we possess by means of which we can trace the connection between his Kantian experience and the genesis of his pessimism. These letters reveal the growth of his despair. The beginnings are seen in the letter of September

18th, which, despite its confident and reassuring tone, testifies to his underlying doubts:

Dass ein Gott sei, dass es ein ewiges Leben, einen Lohn für die Tugend, eine Strafe für das Laster gebe, das alles sind Sätze, die . . . wir also entbehren können. Denn gewiss sollen wir sie nach dem Willen der Gottheit selbst entbehren können, weil sie es uns selbst unmöglich gemacht hat, es einzusehen und zu begreifen.[1] Würdest Du nicht mehr tun, was Recht ist, wenn der Gedanke an Gott und Unsterblichkeit nur ein Traum wäre? Ich nicht. [vi].

Six months later Kleist's confidence has given way to a sense of bewilderment. The positive side of Kant's philosophy has disappeared from his view and he concentrates exclusively on the implications of Kant's epistemology. 'Wir können nicht entscheiden,' he writes on March 22, 1801, with conscious self-dramatization, 'ob das, was wir Wahrheit nennen, wahrhaft Wahrheit ist, oder ob es uns nur so scheint. Ist das letzte, so ist die Wahrheit, die wir hier sammeln, nach dem Tode nicht mehr — und alles Bestreben, ein Eigentum sich zu erwerben, das uns auch in das Grab folgt, ist vergeblich — Ach, Wilhelmine, wenn die Spitze dieses Gedankens Dein Herz nicht trifft, so lächle nicht über einen Andern, der sich tief in seinem heiligsten Innern davon verwundet fühlt. Mein einziges, mein höchstes Ziel ist gesunken, und ich habe nun keines mehr —' [vii].

The letters of July 21 and August 15, 1801, reveal that the ultimate result of Kleist's disillusionment was a dispirited scepticism about the benevolence of God and about the value of human existence:

Das Leben ist das einzige Eigentum, das nur dann etwas wert ist, wenn wir es nicht achten . . . Wer es mit Sorgfalt liebt, moralisch tot ist er schon, denn seine höchste Lebenskraft, nämlich es opfern zu können, modert, indessen er es pflegt. Und doch — o wie unbegreiflich ist der Wille, der über uns waltet! — Dieses rätselhafte Ding, das wir besitzen, wir wissen nicht von wem, das uns fortführt, wir wissen nicht wohin, das unser Eigentum ist, wir wissen nicht, ob wir darüber schalten dürfen, eine Habe, die nichts wert ist, wenn sie uns etwas wert ist, ein Ding, wie ein Widerspruch, flach und tief, öde und reich, würdig und verächtlich, vieldeutig und unergründlich, ein Ding, das jeder wegwerfen mögte, wie ein unverständliches Buch, sind wir nicht durch ein Naturgesetz gezwungen, es zu lieben? [viii].

Ja, wahrlich, wenn man überlegt, dass wir ein Leben bedürfen, um zu lernen, wie wir leben müssten, dass wir selbst im Tode noch nicht ahnden,

---

[1] Note this sentence. It contains Kleist's own reaction to Kant and it is an idea that is foreign to both Kant and Fichte.

was der Himmel mit uns will, wenn niemand den Zweck seines Daseins und seine Bestimmung kennt, wenn die menschliche Vernunft nicht hinreicht, sich und die Seele und das Leben und die Dinge um sich zu begreifen, wenn man seit Jahrtausenden noch zweifelt, ob es ein Recht gibt — kann Gott von solchen Wesen Verantwortlichkeit fordern? . . . Was heisst das auch, etwas Böses tun, der Wirkung nach? Was ist böse? Absolut böse? [ix].

In the *Kritik der praktischen Vernunft*, Kant had defined the true meaning of human freedom and proclaimed the moral responsibility of man. It was not his intention to establish the relativity of all values. 'Eine Relativierung des Wahrheitsbegriffes ist offenbar das genaue Gegenteil von dem, was (die kritische Philosophie) geschichtlich und systematisch erstrebt hat'[1] [x]. Kleist's pessimism embraced the 'phenomenal' as well as the 'noumenal' sphere, a development foreign to the spirit of Kant's philosophy. 'Kant recognizes, indeed, the impossibility of reaching happiness conceived as enjoyment . . . He shows, too, how nature has failed to provide for all the conditions necessary to human felicity. On the other hand, he finds a path of transition from this empirical pessimism to a metaphysical optimism, namely, the recognition of moral freedom as the ultimate and absolute end of the world.'[2] Kleist could not relinquish his belief that happiness was the goal of life, a happiness which he conceived as enjoyment:

Geniessen! Das ist der Preis des Lebens! Ja, wahrlich, wenn wir seiner

---

[1] E. Cassirer, loc. cit., p. 160.

[2] James Sully: *Pessimism*, 1891, p. 67. Nietzsche, like Kleist, recognized the pessimistic and the tragic implications of Kant's theory of knowledge, and his views are of great interest when we consider Kleist's intellectual experiences and the connections between his pessimism and his artistic development: 'Schauen wir, mit gestärkten und an den Griechen erlabten Augen, auf die höchsten Sphären derjenigen Welt, die uns umflutet, so gewahren wir die in Sokrates vorbildlich erscheinende Gier der unersättlichen optimistischen Erkenntnis in tragische Resignation und Kunstbedürftigkeit umgeschlagen' (*Die Geburt der Tragödie*, paragr. 15). 'Der ungeheuren Tapferkeit und Weisheit Kants und Schopenhauers ist der schwerste Sieg gelungen, der Sieg über den im Wesen der Logik verborgen liegenden Optimismus, der wiederum der Untergrund unserer Kultur ist. Wenn dieser an die Erkennbarkeit und Ergründlichkeit aller Welträtsel, gestützt auf die ihm unbedenklichen aeternae veritates, geglaubt, . . . offenbarte Kant, wie diese eigentlich nur dazu dienten, die blosse Erscheinung, das Werk der Maja, zur einzigen und höchsten Realität zu erheben und sie an die Stelle des innersten und wahren Wesens der Dinge zu setzen . . . Mit dieser Erkenntnis ist eine Kultur eingeleitet, welche ich als eine tragische zu bezeichnen wage: deren wichtigstes Merkmal ist, dass an die Stelle der Wissenschaft als höchstes Ziel die Weisheit gerückt wird, die sich, ungetäuscht durch die verführerischen Ablenkungen der Wissenschaften, mit unbewegtem Blicke dem Gesamtbilde der Welt zuwendet und in diesem das ewige Leiden mit sympathischer Liebesempfindung als das eigene Leiden zu ergreifen sucht.' (ibid., paragr. 18). It is, however, worthy of note that Nietzsche himself, in the preface of 1886 to *Die Geburt der Tragödie* recognized 'dass ich mühselig mit Schopenhauerischen und Kantischen Formeln fremde und neue Wertschätzungen auszudrücken suchte, welche dem Geiste Kantens und Schopenhauers, ebenso wie ihrem Geschmacke, von Grund aus entgegen gingen!' [xii].

niemals froh werden, können wir nicht mit Recht den Schöpfer fragen, warum gabst Du es mir? Lebensgenuss seinen Geschöpfen zu geben, das ist die Verpflichtung des Himmels; die Verpflichtung des Menschen ist es, ihn zu verdienen. Ja, es liegt eine Schuld auf den Menschen, etwas Gutes zu tun, verstehe mich recht, ohne figürlich zu reden, schlechthin zu tun. — Ich werde das immer deutlicher und deutlicher einsehen, immer lebhafter und lebhafter fühlen lernen, bis Vernunft und Herz mit aller Gewalt meiner Seele einen Entschluss bewirken. [xi].

In this letter of August 15th, and in those following, particularly that of October 10th, we see the first signs of a calmer outlook in Kleist. 'Seit einigen Wochen,' he writes on August 15th, 'scheint es mir, als hätte sich der Sturm ein wenig gelegt' [xiii]; and on October 10th: 'Indessen fühle ich mich doch wirklich von Tage zu Tage immer heiterer und heiterer, und hoffe, dass endlich die Natur auch mir einmal das Mass von Glück zumessen wird, das sie allen ihren Wesen schuldig ist' [xiv]. The reason for his appeasement is to be found, not so much in a solution of his metaphysical problems, as in his decision to abandon his search for truth and to direct his efforts towards a more practical end: 'Ich habe den Lauf meiner Studien plötzlich unterbrochen, und werde das Versäumte hier nachholen, aber nicht mehr bloss um der Wahrheit willen, sondern für einen menschenfreundlicheren Zweck.' [xv]. 'Ein grosses Bedürfnis ist in mir rege geworden, ohne dessen Befriedigung ich niemals glücklich sein werde; es ist dieses, etwas Gutes zu tun. Ja, ich glaube fast, dass dieses Bedürfnis bis jetzt immer meiner Trauer dunkel zum Grunde lag, und dass ich mich jetzt seiner bloss deutlich bewusst geworden bin. Es liegt eine Schuld auf dem Menschen, die, wie eine Ehrenschuld, jeden, der Ehrgefühl hat, unaufhörlich mahnt.' [xvi].

The project which he had in mind was to settle in Switzerland and to earn his living as a farmer: 'Was meinst Du, Wilhelmine, ich habe noch etwas von meinem Vermögen, wenig zwar, doch wird es hinreichen mir etwa in der Schweiz einen Bauerhof zu kaufen, der mich ernähren kann, wenn ich selbst arbeite.' [xvii]. He pursued this curious notion, in spite of Wilhelmine's justifiable scruples, to the extent of borrowing money from his sister and negotiating for the purchase of a piece of land, but he gave it up for the ostensible reason that the French annexation of Switzerland appeared imminent. 'Es hatte allen Anschein' he wrote to Ulrike on February 19th, 1802, 'dass die Schweiz sowie Cisalpinien, französisch werden wird, und mich ekelt vor dem blossen Gedanken.' [xviii]. But

the whole plan was a chimera, as Kleist well knew, the product
of a desperate effort to find relief from the restlessness that beset
him: 'Ja, was ich sagen wollte,' he wrote to Ulrike on January 12th,
1802, 'ich bin nun einmal so verliebt in den Gedanken, ein Feld zu
bauen, dass es wohl wird geschehen müssen: Betrachte mein Herz
wie einen Kranken, diesen Wunsch wie eine kleine Lüsternheit,
die man, wenn sie unschädlich ist, immerhin gewähren kann. —
Und im Ernste, wenn ich mein letztes Jahr überdenke, wenn ich
erwäge, wie ich so seltsam erbittert gewesen bin gegen mich und
Alles, was mich umgab, so glaube ich fast, dass ich wirklich krank
bin.' [xix]. Perhaps the whole scheme was merely an elaborate
device to escape from his commitments in Germany (including
his engagement to Wilhelmine von Zenge) and to secure for himself
a retreat, in which he could pursue his literary activities undisturbed.
For indeed he knew that in these activities lay his only hope of
salvation. The last letter which he wrote to Wilhelmine von Zenge,
in reply to her exhortation to him to return to Germany, contains
his honest confession of the motives that prompted him. It is dated
May 20, 1802.

'Ich werde,' he writes, 'wahrscheinlicher Weise niemals in mein Vaterland
zurückkehren. Ihr Weiber versteht in der Regel ein Wort in der deutschen
Sprache nicht, es heisst Ehrgeiz. Es ist nur ein einziger Fall in welchem
ich zurückkehre, wenn ich der Erwartung der Menschen, die ich törigter
Weise durch eine Menge von prahlerischen Schritten gereizt habe, ent-
sprechen kann. Der Fall ist möglich, aber nicht wahrscheinlich. Kurz,
kann ich nicht mit Ruhm im Vaterland erscheinen, geschieht es nie. Das
ist entschieden, wie die Natur meiner Seele.' [xx].

Six months later he did, in fact, return to Germany. He had been
'saved' from utter despair and from the paralysis of his spiritual powers
not by his enterprises in philosophy, nor by his romantic notions of
tilling the soil, but by his ambition to become a great writer, to wrest,
as he said, the laurels of poetry from the brows of Goethe. His
beginnings as a writer are the product of his intellectual disillusionment, coupled with his desire to prove his own worth. His inspiration,
if this term is applicable in his case, represents a mixture of bitter
recrimination against life and proud self-justification.

3

When we read the letters which Kleist wrote during the years 1800
to 1802, the formative years of his literary career, to his most intimate

friends and relations, to whom he freely reported his spiritual difficulties and his material cares, we are struck by his reticence concerning his activities as a poet. About his beginnings as a writer we know
less than about those of any other great author of his time. In Paris
Kleist struggled passionately to complete his drama *Robert Guiskard*,
but there is no unambiguous mention of this side of his life in his
letters from that city. The processes of his poetic creation at this
stage are a secret that cannot be unravelled by psychological analysis.
The mystery is shrouded impenetrably. How could his 'Kantian
experience' supply the impetus that turned him from an earnest
seeker of truth pursuing the ideal of self-perfection, the believer in
universal harmony, into a poet whose inspiration lay in the recognition of human fallibility and of the uncertainty of life? We cannot
explain the fact that the Kleist of the 'Lebensplan' showed no signs
of his poetic vocation, that he has left few traces of literary apprenticeship and that in a short time he stood revealed as a poet of remarkable
originality and power. What little evidence there is, may be found
in his letters to Wilhelmine from Lungwitz and Würzburg in
September and October, 1800. We catch glimpses of the future
dramatist in the snatches of conversation which he reproduced in
dialogue in these letters. In themselves these passages are insignificant,
but they indicate Kleist's tendency towards dramatic representation.
Another instance is seen in the description of the inmates of the
Würzburg asylum, particularly that of a young man whom Kleist
professes to have observed. It has been shown by medical experts[1]
that this experience was a piece of invention by Kleist and his
description should therefore be regarded as a literary exercise. A
third example is found in the remarkably vivid and appealing evoca-
tion of a scene in the Hameau de Chantilly which he gives in his
letters to Luise von Zenge on August 16, 1801. The depiction
of this lovers' idyll bears every trace of being another piece of
imaginative writing and it reminds us of the lovers' episodes in *Die
Familie Schroffenstein*, on which Kleist was then working.

Finally, an indication of Kleist's beginnings as a writer may be
sought in those passages in his letters of October 11, 1800 and of
May 21 and July 18, 1801, in which he describes the course of
certain rivers in similar, if not identical terms.[2] In each instance his

---

[1] Cf. M. Morris: *H. v. Kleists Reise nach Würzburg*, 1899, p. 28, and S. Rahmer: *Das Kleist-
Problem*, 1903, Ch. 3.
[2] For other instances of this kind see the letters of September 4, 1800, January 21, 1801
and August 16, 1801.

attention was arrested by the river's circumvention of an obstacle
and in each case he uses an image drawn from the sphere of human
relationships in order to indicate the significance of the scene. These
passages are of some interest in assessing the quality of Kleist's poetic
imagination. At the time when he wrote them, at the beginning,
therefore, of his literary apprenticeship, he was busy compiling an
'Ideenmagazin' in which he recorded the analogies between natural
and psychological phenomena. The predominantly intellectual
quality of his imagery derives from this passion for analogy and it
forms a striking contrast, at this stage, as well as in his mature work,
with the profoundly irrational aspects of his poetry.

(1) Besonders ein Schauspiel ist mir sehr merkwürdig. Grade aus
strömt der Main von der Brücke weg, und pfeilschnell, als hätte er sein
Ziel schon im Auge, als sollte ihn nichts abhalten, es zu erreichen, als wollte
er es, ungeduldig, auf dem kürzesten Wege ereilen — aber ein Rebenhügel beugt seinen stürmischen Lauf, sanft aber mit festem Sinn, wie eine
Gattin den stürmischen Willen ihres Mannes, und zeigt ihm mit edler
Standhaftigkeit den Weg, der ihn ins Meer führen wird — und er ehrt die
bescheidne Warnung und folgt der freundlichen Weisung, und gibt sein
voreiliges Ziel auf und durchbricht den Rebenhügel nicht, sondern um-
geht ihn, mit beruhigtem Laufe, seine blumigen Füsse ihm küssend —.
(October 11, 1800).

(2) Dresden hat eine grosse, feierliche Lage, in der Mitte der umkränzen-
den Elbhöhen, die in einiger Entfernung, als ob sie aus Ehrfurcht nicht näher
zu treten wagten, es umlagern. Der Strom verlässt plötzlich sein rechtes
Ufer, und wendet sich schnell nach Dresden, seinen Liebling zu küssen.
Von der Höhe des Zwingers kann man seinen Lauf fast bis nach Meissen
verfolgen. Er wendet sich bald zu dem rechten, bald zu dem linken Ufer,
als würde die Wahl ihm schwer, und wankt, wie vor Entzücken, und
schlängelt sich spielend in tausend Umwegen durch das freundliche Tal,
als wollte er nicht in das Meer. (May 21, 1801). Later in this letter Kleist
describes the Elbe entering the Erzgebirge at Losowitz:
Wie eine Jungfrau unter Männern erscheint, so tritt sie schlank und klar
unter die Felsen — Leise mit schüchternem Wanken naht sie sich — das
rohe Geschlecht drängt sich, den Weg ihr versperrend, um sie herum,
der Glänzend-Reinen ins Antlitz zu schauen — sie aber ohne zu harren,
windet sich, flüchtig, errötend, hindurch —

(3) In the letter of July 18, 1801, we have the same description of the
Elbe at Dresden as that above, and then the following addition:
Und die Weissritz, die sich aus den Tiefen des plauenschen Grundes
losringt, wie ein verstohlnes Gefühl aus der Tiefe der Brust, die, immer an
Felsen wie an Vorurteilen sich stossend, nicht zornig, aber doch ein wenig

unwillig murmelt, sich unermüdet durch alle Hindernisse windet, bis sie
an die Freiheit des Tages tritt und sich ausbreitet in dem offnen Felde und
frei und ruhig ihrer Bestimmung gemäss ins Meer fliesst —
Later in this letter we find a description of the Rhine in the identical words
Kleist had used for the Main on October 11, 1800, and then the following
addition:

Aber still und breit und majestätisch strömt er bei Bingen heran, und
sicher, wie ein Held zum Siege, und langsam, als ob er seine Bahn wohl
vollenden würde — und ein Gebirge (der Hundsrück) wirft sich ihm in den
Weg, wie die Verläumdung der unbescholtenen Tugend. Er aber durchbricht es, und wankt nicht, und die Felsen weichen ihm aus, und blicken
mit Bewunderung und Erstaunen auf ihn hinab — doch er eilt verächtlich
bei ihnen vorüber, aber ohne zu frohlocken, und die einzige Rache, die er
sich erlaubt, ist diese, ihnen in seinem klaren Spiegel ihr schwarzes Bild zu
zeigen — [xxi].

The courses of great rivers clearly possessed symbolical value for
Kleist as they did for Hölderlin, and the direction of his mind at the
time when his poetic faculty was aroused is seen in his choice of this
symbol. The differences between the earlier and the later descriptions,
between those written before his reading of Kant and those after it,
i.e. before and after 1800, are perhaps more significant than the
similarities, and they help us to uncover, if not completely, the
sources of his poetic inspiration.

In the first passage, written in Würzburg, the symbolism is purely
sexual. The point of reference is clearly Kleist's relation with his
bride and his description illuminates his personal problem in this
relationship.[1] The problem had a bearing on his future development as
a poet and it is perhaps the root of the difficulties which he then rational-
ized in terms of his Kantian experience. It is thus significant that he
modified the sexual symbolism in the letter of May 21st. His
estrangement from Wilhelmine and his escape from entanglements
in Germany give us the key to the understanding of the symbol in
this letter. The symbolism is finally altered in the later passage of
the same letter, for now the river is made to represent not the sexual
desires of a man, but the behaviour of a virgin, the rocks signifying

[1] Cf. his use of the image in his early poem *Für Wilhelmine von Zenge*. Speaking of love
he says:

> Sie muss des Wankelmutes Sandbank meiden,
> Geschickt des Misstrauns spitzen Fels umgehn,
> Und mit des Schicksals wilden Wogen kämpfen,
> Bis in des Glückes sichern Port sie läuft. [xxii].

This is an allegorical adaptation of what had originally been an experience possessing
symbolical significance.

not, as before, the woman's restraint upon sexual impulses, but those impulses themselves. In speaking of the Weissritz in his letter to Karoline von Schlieben on July 18, 1801, Kleist changes the sexual urge, which he retained in the earlier part of his description, into the more general 'verstohlenes Gefühl' and the opposing force now is prejudice, the goal being freedom. The use of the symbol is here conditioned by Kleist's view of human relationships after his reading of Kant. The same is true of his description of the Rhine in this letter, with the difference that victory and triumph are the key-notes here rather than escape. It is significant, too, that the obstacles thwarting the Weissritz and the Rhine are, respectively, prejudice and calumny, so that a source of Kleist's inspiration appears to be his distrust of human beings, a feeling engendered in him by his interpretation of Kant's epistemology.

In his description of the Rhine Kleist expressed his attitude to life at the beginning of his literary career, his morbid fears and his resolve to win the admiration of his fellow-men — 'aber ohne zu frohlocken, und die einzige Rache, die er sich erlaubt, ist diese, ihnen in seinem klaren Spiegel ihr schwarzes Bild zu zeigen.' From his descriptions of the Elbe and the Rhine, also, two figures emerge—the pure maiden and the triumphant hero. They are Kleist's dramatic archetypes. In contrast to them are those figures whose prejudices and suspicions assail the integrity of the heroes' character. Kleist's symbolism in his letters enables us to gain an insight into his most formative period as a writer and to lay bare the rudiments of his first completed drama, *Die Familie Schroffenstein*.

There is one aspect of Kleist's early dramas which is not represented in his descriptions of the rivers. In his tragedies the suspicions of the parties opposing each other are the result of an inherent weakness of human nature, the inability to distinguish the true from the false, but ultimately the responsibility for the ensuing misfortunes lies with Fate rather than with the human beings. The prejudices engendered in men are provoked by an incalculable higher being. The genesis of this thought has already been traced in Kleist's letters and it is of great importance in his tragedies. His dramatic work from *Robert Guiskard* to *Penthesilea* represents the combination of this theme with the view of life indicated in his use of the river symbol, but the symbol itself does not represent this theme.

It is surprising that in Kleist's dramas we do not find any striking instances of his use of the river symbol. This may be explained by the fact that the symbol did not fully express his attitude to life, for it did not include the notion that human suffering is caused by the intervention of a superior power. An image that we do find in his dramas expressed his fundamental feeling more adequately. It occurs in *Die Familie Schroffenstein*:

> Freilich mag
> Wohl mancher sinken, weil er stark ist: Denn
> Die kranke, abgestorbne Eiche steht
> Dem Sturm, doch die gesunde stürzt er nieder,
> Weil er in ihre Krone greifen kann. [xxiii].

and in the concluding words of *Penthesilea*:

> Sie sank, weil sie zu stolz und kräftig blühte!
> Die abgestorbne Eiche steht im Sturm,
> Doch die gesunde stürzt er schmetternd nieder,
> Weil er in ihre Krone greifen kann. [xxiv]

The image of the oak tree which is laid low by the tempest because its growth had been too strong and too luxuriant is particularly significant, since it aptly represents Kleist's conception of the tragedy of human life.[1] Other images occurring in Kleist's work and possessing symbolical significance are the vaulted gateway, and the bathing stag. There are many quite commonplace images in his writings, while others are devoid of poetic value since they owe their existence to Kleist's peculiarly intellectual and deliberate method of collecting data for his 'Ideenmagazin'. In his letter to Wilhelmine von Zenge from Berlin on November 18, 1800, he urges his bride to imitate his own practice of reflecting upon interesting natural and other phenomena with a view to discovering their wider significance:

> Bemühe Dich also von jetzt an, recht aufmerksam zu sein, auf alle Erscheinungen, die Dich umgeben. Keine ist unwichtig, jede, auch die scheinbar unbedeutendste, enthält doch etwas, das merkwürdig ist, wenn wir es nur wahrzunehmen wissen. Aber bestrebe Dich, nicht bloss die Erscheinungen wahrzunehmen, sondern auch etwas von ihnen zu lernen. Frage bei jeder Erscheinung entweder: worauf deutet das hin? und dann wird die Antwort Dich mit irgend einer nützlichen Lehre bereichern; oder frage wenigstens, wenn das nicht geht: womit hat dies eine Ähnlichkeit? und dann wird das Auffinden des Gleichnisses wenigstens Deinen Verstand schärfen [xxv].

'Du weisst' he writes at the end of the letter, 'dass ich mich jetzt für das schriftstellerische Fach bilde. Ich selbst habe mir schon ein

[1] Otto Ludwig borrowed this image from Kleist when discussing the difference between characters of novels and those of dramas. (Cf. *Schriften*, ed. Schmidt, Vol. VI, p. 168.)

B

kleines Ideenmagazin angelegt . . .' [xxvi]. It was typical of Kleist that he approached the task of authorship in such a methodical manner at a stage in his career when the ideals of 'Bildung' were still paramount and before he suffered the reversal of having these ideals upset by Kant. In assessing his value as a poet the intellectual component in his work should always be remembered. 'Tanto intellettualistico' says Benedetto Croce 'è il procedere del Kleist che sovente non può evitare la banalità e superficialità e puerilità della trattazione . . . Le sue doti erano secondarie, doti proprie degli oratori, cioè chiarezza nella esposizione drammatica, vivezza descrittiva, energia di tono; ma forse non v'ha in lui un sol luogo veramente poetico.'[1] On the other hand the profoundly pathological and the undeniably poetic quality of his genius should not be overlooked, nor does Croce overlook it, without, however, attempting to relate together the two aspects of Kleist's mind and to acknowledge the peculiar values of his art.

In his persistent use of certain images we may discover a symbolical significance and find a key to understanding the fusion of Kleist's intellectual powers with the pathological forces that also governed him. His images are vivid and lucid and their symbolical application is characterized by a careful, almost logical employment of detail. In this aspect his imagery reveals the results of his training when he compiled his Magazine of Ideas. At the same time those images which are symbolically significant bear traces of their origins in Kleist's irrational attitude to life, in his distrust of the powers which, he believed, thwarted the happiness of man, or in his own sexual frustrations. The image of the oak in the storm is an instance of the first kind. Another is the metaphor of the vaulted gateway, the significance of which will be examined in the chapter on *Penthesilea*. A third example, more clearly revealing the sexual origin of Kleist's imagery, is found in his use of the picture of the bathing stag.

In the important letter written to Wilhelmine in Paris on July 21, 1801, in which he discusses the causes and the effects of his spiritual predicament, he concludes his account with a desperate cry for relief:

Geduld — es wird nicht immer so sein, und ich sehne mich nach einem Tage, wie der Hirsch in der Mittagshitze nach dem Strome, sich hineinzustürzen. — Aber Geduld! — Geduld? — Kann der Himmel die von seinen Menschen verlangen, da er ihnen selbst ein Herz voll Sehnsucht gab? Zerstreuung! Zerstreuung! [xxvii].

[1] *Poesia e Non Poesia*, 1923, p. 56 p.

The spiritual cause of Kleist's malaise is clearly expressed in this
passage, but its physical counterpart and the remedy which he envisaged and desired are not unequivocally stated. They reveal themselves when we note the use of the image of the stag in *Käthchen von
Heilbronn*. In this drama Wetter vom Strahl, when he is at last free
to marry Käthchen, speaks to her as follows:

> Zuerst, mein süsses Kind, muss ich dir sagen,
> Dass ich mit Liebe dir, unsäglich, ewig,
> Durch alle meine Sinne zugetan.
> Der Hirsch, der, von der Mittagsglut gequält,
> Den Grund zerwühlt, mit spitzigem Geweih,
> Er sehnt sich so begierig nicht,
> Vom Felsen in den Waldstrom sich zu stürzen,
> Den reissenden, als ich, jetzt, da du mein bist,
> In alle deine jungen Reize mich. [xxviii].[1]

This passage demonstrates the fusion of Kleist's intellectual powers
with his irrational impulses in the production of poetry. His imagery
reveals his profounder desires as well as his ability to transpose with
logical exactitude a wealth of detail from observed reality into the
realm of symbolical meaning.

Kleist's view of tragedy combined two opposite notions, and in his
dramas two different conceptions of the tragic may be found. On the
one hand tragic happenings are for him the result of human weakness,
of the fallibility of human reason and human feelings; on the other
hand they are the product of the exalted strength of human passion
which provokes the intervention of a higher power in the life of those
who experience this passion, and causes their tragic destruction.
The combination of these opposite notions in his most characteristic
tragedies, in *Amphitryon* and in *Penthesilea*, is Kleist's distinctive
contribution to the genre.

When intellectual pessimism began to spread in Germany in the
last quarter of the eighteenth century, many writers found comfort
in Rousseau's doctrine of the value of passion. The dramatists of the
'Sturm und Drang' represented this aspect of the reaction against the
intellectual optimism of the previous era, and in this respect Kleist

---

[1] For a similar use of this image, see Ventidius' words to Thusnelda in *Die Hermannsschlacht*.

> Wie mild der Mondschein durch die Stämme fällt!
> Und wie der Waldbach fern, mit üppigem Geplätscher,
> Vom Rand des hohen Felsens niederrinnt! —
> Thusnelda! Komm und lösche diese Glut,
> Soll ich, gleich einem jungen Hirsch,
> Das Haupt voran, mich in die Flut nicht stürzen! [xxix].

is their true successor. His letters to Wilhelmine von Zenge reveal his admiration for Rousseau, and indeed his plan to settle in Switzerland as a peasant is partly inspired by Rousseau's writings. Similarly, he is a disciple of Rousseau when he makes this statement in his letter of January 21, 1801: 'Grosse Empfindungen zeigen eine starke, umfassende Seele an. Wo der Wind das Meer nur flüchtig kräuselt, da ist es flach, aber wo er die Wellen türmt, da ist es tief.' [xxx]. His view is sharply contrasted with the stoic ideal which Winckelmann expressed when he wrote: 'So wie die Tiefe des Meeres allezeit ruhig bleibt, die Oberfläche mag noch so wüten, ebenso zeigt der Ausdruck in den Figuren der Griechen bei allen Leidenschaften eine grosse und gesetzte Seele.' [xxxi][1]. Kleist was in agreement with Lessing's opposition to this view, as he stated it in *Laokoon*, and however much his conception of tragedy differs from Lessing's, he, too, rejected the ideal of stoicism. Sylvester's words in *Die Familie Schroffenstein* make this clear:

> Nicht jeden Schlag ertragen soll der Mensch,
> Und welchen Gott fasst, denk' ich, der darf sinken,
> — Auch seufzen. Denn der Gleichmut ist die Tugend
> Nur der Athleten. Wir, wir Menschen fallen
> Ja nicht für Geld, auch nicht zur Schau. — Doch sollen
> Wir stets des Anschauns würdig aufstehn. [xxxii].

Tragic sublimity for Kleist resides in the capacity of experiencing great passions, but with dignity. His most tragic characters, Alkmene and Penthesilea, are sublime because they are endowed with great emotions and they are tragic because, by virtue of these emotions, they become the victims of higher powers. The storm of Fate destroys them because they possess exalted qualities, in excess of those which enable lesser men and women to live in obscurity and hence in safety. This view of tragedy resembles Hebbel's conception, rather than that of Schiller, whose classical drama represents a return to the ideal of stoic 'Gleichmut'. In Schiller weakness of character, the flaw in the great individual's armour, exposes the hero to the blows of Fate. In Kleist it is man's exalted strength that attracts the storm which overwhelms him with disaster.

The difference between Kleist and Schiller is clearly revealed in their attitudes to the function of the sublime in tragedy. Schiller based his views on Kant's *Kritik der Urteilskraft*. For him, as for Kant, true sublimity resides not so much in the grandeur of physical or emotional power, as in the supremacy of the spirit of man over this

---

[1] *Kleine Schriften und Briefe*, ed. H. Uhde-Bernays, Vol. I, p. 81.

power. 'Also ist die Erhabenheit' says Kant[1] 'in keinem Dinge der Natur, sondern nur in unserem Gemüte enthalten, sofern wir der Natur in uns, und dadurch der Natur . . . ausser uns überlegen zu sein uns bewusst werden können.' [xxxiii]. This view finds its echo in Schiller: 'Innere Gemütsfreiheit gehört schlechterdings dazu, um das Furchtbare erhaben zu finden und Wohlgefallen daran zu haben; denn es kann ja bloss dadurch erhaben sein, dass es unsere Unabhängigkeit, unsere Gemütsfreiheit zu empfinden gibt.' [xxxiv].[2]

The sublime had another meaning for Kleist. In his letter to Ulrike on May 1, 1802 he made the characteristic statement: 'Das Leben hat doch immer nichts Erhabeneres, als nur dieses, dass man es erhaben wegwerfen kann.' [xxxv] When the powers of Fate proved overwhelming, he envisaged the self-obliteration of man with a gesture of sublime contempt, whereas Schiller saw in such an eventuality an opportunity for the sublime ascendancy of the moral principle in man. In Kleist's tragedies the powers that destroy man remain triumphant, in Schiller we are consoled by the display of human independence within distress.

In his view of the sublime Kleist was in agreement with Burke rather than with Kant. 'Whatever is fitted in any sort' Burke wrote 'to excite the ideas of pain and danger, that is to say, whatever is in any sort terrible, or is conversant about terrible objects, or operates in a manner analogous to terror, is a source of the sublime; that is, it is productive of the strongest emotion which the mind is capable of feeling.'[3] It is probable that Kleist became acquainted with this view in 1807 or 1808 through Adam Müller, who greatly admired Burke and wished to influence Kleist's literary production.[4] At that time Kleist had not completed *Penthesilea* and while only indirect evidence can be adduced to prove that this tragedy owed anything to Burke's treatise, it is to this treatise rather than to Kant's theory that we may look for an explanation of Kleist's view of the ultimate function of tragedy.

In his tragedies the excitement of terror is not mitigated, as it is in those of Goethe and Schiller who agreed with the precepts of the *Hamburgische Dramaturgie* on the subject of the tragic emotions and of Katharsis, although they also disagreed with Lessing on important issues. Lessing demonstrated the necessity of reducing the intensity of tragic suffering through the excitement of pity and fear rather than

---

[1] Kritik der Urteilskraft, § 28.   [2] Werke, Säkularausgabe, Vol. XII, p. 301.
[3] A Philosophical Inquiry on the Origin of our Ideas of the Sublime and Beautiful, Pt. I, Sect. 7.
[4] Cf. G. Stefansky: Ein neuer Weg zu Heinrich von Kleist, Euphorion, Vol. XXIII, p. 639 passim.

pity and terror, and through the purification of these emotions by means of Katharsis. Schiller's principle of moderation is contained, among others, in the following lines from *Über naive und sentimentalische Dichtung*: 'Diese Freiheit des Gemüts in uns hervorzubringen und zu nähren, ist die schöne Aufgabe der Komödie, so wie die Tragödie bestimmt ist, die Gemütsfreiheit, wenn sie durch einen Affekt gewaltsam aufgehoben worden, auf ästhetischem Weg wieder herstellen zu helfen.' [xxxvi].[1] Goethe interprets the term Katharsis as 'Ausgleichung' and 'aussöhnende Abrundung, welche eigentlich von allem Drama, ja sogar von allen poetischen Werken gefordert wird.' 'Eine Söhnung, eine Lösung ist zum Abschluss unerlässlich, wenn die Tragödie ein vollkommenes Dichtwerk sein soll.' [xxxvii].[2]

Even in his tragic dramas Kleist clearly endeavoured to conform to this principle. A cathartic effect, as Goethe envisaged it, is produced, e.g., in *Penthesilea*, but Kleist's dramas are nevertheless in spirit entirely opposed to Goethe's conception of the function of tragedy. His tragedies possess the radical quality which Lessing endeavoured to banish from the German theatre and which Goethe and Schiller condemned. They were born of despair and so they enforce rather than purify or neutralize the ideas of pain and danger which are, according to Burke, a primary source of the sublime. Kleist's sense of the tragic was uncompromising, for he was not able to resolve the disharmonies of life by trusting, as did Lessing, Goethe and Schiller, in a cosmic order of harmony. The divine balance of things in which they believed, was for him disturbed by an incomprehensible power. These writers played a part in the formulation and development of Idealist views in Germany. For Kleist the premisses of that creed were unacceptable, as soon as he had encountered and, in his individual way, absorbed Kant's philosophy of the *Critique of Pure Reason*.

4

We are now able to define more carefully the essential difference between Grillparzer's and Kleist's pessimism. For both dramatists the source of human tragedy lay in human nature, but whereas for Grillparzer the responsibility rested almost entirely with man by refusing to assert his will-power at the right time, to overcome temptation by making the right choice, for Kleist tragedy lay in man's inability to distinguish between the true and the untrue, an

---

[1] *Werke, Säkularausgabe*, Vol. XII, pp. 197 f.
[2] *Nachlese zu Aristoteles Poetik, Über Kunst und Altertum* 1827.

incapacity inherent in his very nature. In the last resort Grillparzer, as his letters and diaries show, based his view of tragedy on an analysis of his own character, on self-criticism.[1] His presentation of human weakness in his dramas is a generalization of his self-accusations and it is centred upon a recognition of human responsibility. In Kleist's pessimism there is scarcely a trace of self-criticism. Human fallibility, the weakness of man's cognitive faculties, is a fault for which man cannot be held responsible. Like Thomas Hardy he blamed an inscrutable higher force for the ravages of human life. Man is the victim of Fate and in the battle of life his powers are crippled from the start. He is blinded before the battle begins and in his mistaken efforts to achieve self-realization he destroys his fellow-men and is destroyed by them.

When Grillparzer's characters err, they do so because they desire more for themselves than is their due. They are noble men and women betrayed by their ambitions. They delude themselves, but, with few exceptions, they are not misled by their fellow-men. Kleist's characters err because they cannot understand the desires of others. They are not suspicious of their own motives, but suspect those of their fellow-men, and such is the ill-fated constellation of events in their lives, that they cannot know the correct facts of the situation or judge the behaviour of other characters. With few exceptions they misinterpret each others' actions, because they lack faith and trust in one another. Kleist regarded mutual trust as the indispensable condition of human relationships. He reiterated his belief in many letters to Wilhelmine and appealed to her for understanding at times when she had good cause to suspect his behaviour towards her. In this sense Kleist envisaged the necessity of human responsibility. At the same time his demand for confidence reveals the essential egotism of his principles. It is not a purely ethical concept and it does not possess the virtue of arising from self-criticism, which characterizes Grillparzer's ethical demands.

Kleist only rarely makes his characters analyse their own motives or justify their own behaviour, as an examination of his use of monologues and dialogues in his dramas will show. He used the monologue not as other dramatists do, in order to reveal the deeper springs of self-doubt and hesitation in the principal characters, but as a means of exposing their growing suspicion and distrust of others, for example in *Amphitryon*. Indeed, monologues occur rarely in Kleist's

---

[1] Cf. Edna Purdie: *Two nineteenth-century Diaries and their Writers. Publ. of the Engl. Goethe Soc.*, 1946, pp. 21 ff.

tragedies. In his most characteristic works they are the exception rather than the rule.

In the seventeenth century a strong opposition is found in the writings of French critics to the use of monologues, since the practice of making characters speak their thoughts aloud conflicted with the principle of 'vraisemblance'. Gottsched shared this view in the eighteenth century, but his precepts had little influence on the German theatre. Kleist's uncompromising realism, his desire to produce utter psychological veracity, made him agree with Gottsched on this point, and on this point alone, and although it is unlikely that he carefully read the *Critische Dichtkunst* he was, in this respect, the first important dramatist in Germany to conform to Gottsched's principle.

Another reason for Kleist's infrequent use of monologues may be sought in a different aspect of his poetic genius. His work is singularly lacking in lyric qualities.[1] Not only are the drama and the 'Novelle' the only literary forms which he practised with success—his poetry was purely occasional and epigrammatic and possesses little merit—but in his dramas and in his prose writings themselves there is scant evidence of an interest in lyric values which are so prominent in the work of Goethe and not absent from the rhetorical verse of Schiller. In the monologue the lyric genius of a dramatist finds its most convenient outlet and those dramas which treat preeminently the theme of a great character in spiritual conflict with himself, such as *Hamlet* and *Iphigenie auf Tauris*, possess the highest lyric value and give the greatest scope for the use of soliloquies. The conflicts of Kleist's characters, as we have seen, are not of this order. He presented characters in conflict not with themselves, but with others. Their attention is fixed on the minds and the actions of their partners and their adversaries, and they are not given an opportunity to examine their own minds, absorbed as they are in discovering the motives of their antagonists.

In his dramas Kleist created unique characters. Completely certain of the justness of their own motives, never wavering in their judgments, they pursue their cause with fanatical tenaciousness, until, in the tragic catastrophe or in the dramatic solution, their mistakes are revealed. Rupert and Sylvester, Amphitryon and Alkmene, Penthesilea and Achilles, Käthchen and Wetter vom Strahl, Homburg and even the Kurfürst are such characters; and although Kleist's dramas contain more than the conflicts between these pairs of opponents, each

---

[1] M. Praz gives a totally wrong impression of *Penthesilea* when he describes it as a 'lyrical' drama (*The Romantic Agony*, English translation, p. 10).

entrenched in his own position,[1] those conflicts are the core of his dramatic compositions. This point is substantiated by the fact that Kleist, when he revised his dramas for publication, frequently changed soliloquies into dialogues, a tendency found more often in his later than in his earlier plays.[2]

His dialogues, therefore, possess a unique quality. Clemens Brentano remarked in a letter to Arnim: 'Was den Kleist besonders kurios macht, ist sein Rezept zum Dialog. Er denkt sich alle Personen halb taub und dämlich, so kömmt dann durch Fragen und Repetieren der Dialog heraus.' [xxxviii]. Kleist's figures are engrossed in their own thoughts and feelings, they do not listen to the arguments of those with whom they are speaking. Hence their speeches often are not dialogues in the accepted sense of the term. His dramas at their climax frequently give an impression of presenting a series of self-contained, rather than inter-related exchanges of thought and feeling. For this reason, too, there are very few examples of real stichomythia in his plays. He does not often employ that kind of repartee which consists in the rapid reaction of one character to the thought or the feeling of another. In order, then, to represent adequately the peculiar conflicts which he wished to portray, Kleist made little use of monologues and devised a novel form of dialogue.

In this respect there is a considerable amount of similarity between Otto Ludwig's work and that of Kleist. Otto Ludwig defended the use of monologues in the presentation of an 'inner' conflict, i.e. in the exposition of a character divided against itself:

Alle grosse Leidenschaft isoliert. Sie verbirgt sich der Umgebung und sucht die Einsamkeit mit sich selbst zu streiten, sich zu bedauern, sich anzufeuern, mit sich zu beraten, sich schlecht zu machen, sich zu trösten, sich auszutoben . . . Die Entwicklung eines interessanten Charakters ist nur in Monologen möglich. [xxxix].[3]

Such conflicts are to be found in *Die Pfarrrose* and *Das Fräulein von Scuderi* and here Ludwig made extensive use of monologues, particularly in the latter play. In *Der Erbförster* and, to a lesser extent in *Die Makkabäer*, however, we have the self-assured, fanatical characters whom we meet in Kleist's tragedies, and in *Der Erbförster* an atmosphere of suspicion and fatefulness so characteristic of Kleist's dramatic productions. Here the technique adopted by Ludwig resembles that

---

[1] Cf. the different themes treated in such characters as Agnes and Ottokar, Jupiter, Kunigunde, Natalie, etc.
[2] Cf. T. Kaiser: *Vergleich der verschiedenen Fassungen von Kleists Dramen*, 1944, p. 80.
[3] *Schriften*, ed. Schmidt, Vol. V, p. 203.

of Kleist. He uses monologues only on two occasions in *Die Makkabäer* and omits them entirely in *Der Erbförster*.

There is another striking resemblance between Kleist and Otto Ludwig. Both dramatists possessed to an unusual degree a knowledge of music, and music was a source of their inspiration. In a letter dated August, 1811, Kleist wrote: 'So habe ich von meiner frühesten Jugend an alles Allgemeine, was ich über die Dichtkunst gedacht habe, auf Töne bezogen. Ich glaube, dass im Generalbass die wichtigsten Aufschlüsse über die Dichtkunst enthalten sind.' [xl]. Otto Ludwig gives the following account of his 'Verfahren beim poetischen Schaffen':

> Es geht eine Stimmung voraus, eine musikalische, die wird mir zur Farbe, dann seh' ich Gestalten, eine oder mehrere in irgend einer Stellung und Gebärdung für sich oder gegeneinander . . . Wunderlicherweise ist jenes Bild oder jene Gruppe gewöhnlich nicht das Bild der Katastrophe, manchmal nur eine charakteristische Figur in irgend einer pathetischen Stellung, an diese schliesst sich aber sogleich eine ganze Reihe, und vom Stücke erfahr' ich nicht die Fabel, den novellistischen Inhalt zuerst, sondern bald nach vorwärts, bald nach dem Ende zu von der erst gesehenen Situation aus, schiessen immer neue plastisch-mimische Gestalten und Gruppen an, bis ich das ganze Stück in allen seinen Szenen habe. [xli].[1]

Kleist's methods of composition appear to have been the same as those here described by Ludwig. His dramas are, like those of Ludwig, an agglomeration of individual scenes developed from a single situation initially visualized. In the case of *Der Zerbrochene Krug* we know that an engraving by Jean Jaques Le Veau depicting a scene in a court room supplied Kleist with his starting point, and of *Die Familie Schroffenstein* his friend Pfuel, according to Wilbrandt, reports as follows:

> (Kleist) war eines Tages die seltsame Auskleideszene des letzten Aktes, rein als Szene, in den Sinn gekommen und da die Situation ihn anzog, hatte er sie wie eine zusammenhanglose Phantasie niedergeschrieben. Dann erst fiel ihm ein, sie mit andern Fäden der Erfindung, vielleicht auch

---

[1] *Schriften*, ed. Stern and Schmidt, Vol. VI, pp. 215 f. Cf. J. Petersen: *Heinrich von Kleist und Torquato Tasso, Zeitschrift für deutschen Unterricht*, Vol. XXXI, p. 352. Ludwig aptly described Kleist's language as 'Musik des Gedankens' (*Shakespeare Studien*, ed. Heydrich, 1874, p. 348). Cf. Schiller's accounts of his own creative process, 'Die Empfindung ist bei mir anfangs ohne bestimmten und klaren Gegenstand; dieser bildet sich erst später. Eine gewisse musikalische Gemütsstimmung geht vorher, und auf diese folgt bei mir erst die poetische Idee.' 'Das Musikalische eines Gedichts schwebt mir weit öfter vor der Seele, wenn ich mich hinsetze, es zu machen, als der klare Begriff vom Inhalt, über den ich oft kaum mit mir einig bin.' (Letter to Körner, May 25, 1792) [xlii]. The visual experience is not important in the initial stages of Schiller's creative process, whereas it plays a significant part in that of Kleist and Otto Ludwig. For a detailed discussion of this problem see articles by W. Silz listed in the bibliography.

mit einem zufällig entdeckten Stoff . . zusammenzuspinnen, und so wob sich allmählich um diese Szene die ganze Tragödie herum. [xliii].[1]

This method of composition accounts for the weakness of the dramatic plots in the work of both Kleist and Otto Ludwig.

It is difficult for us to visualize together both aspects of Kleist's method of composition, to correlate the musical and the scenic origins of his dramas. As finished products, however, his plays reveal two features which the double source of his inspiration made possible, a musical texture and what Goethe called a 'dialectic', a 'stationäre Prozessform'.

Kleist's dramas usually begin with a prelude stating the principal themes of the work. To these themes the term 'Leitmotive' has been frequently applied. Then follows the development leading to the climax and to the finale.[2] The classical principles of dramatic construction, the succession of exposition, complication, climax, dénouement and catastrophe are not followed in these dramas. What is normally called an exposition is rarely found in Kleist's most characteristic work. Instead of opening his plays with scenes that explore the circumstances preceding the tragic entanglement, in his most significant plays he introduced at the beginning a mysterious event designed to confuse the reader rather than to enlighten him, and this secret dominates the dramatic action until the tragic complications are fully developed. The exposition of antecedent events, e.g. the explanation of Peter's death in *Die Familie Schroffenstein* or the account of the Amazon state in *Penthesilea*, comes much later and sheds a backward rather than a forward light on the action. Similarly, he begins his tragedies, in most cases, at a point of the action when the principal conflict has already set in, not, as Goethe and Schiller did, at a stage antecedent to the inception of the conflict proper.

The plots of Kleist's dramas have therefore been compared to those of detective stories[3] or to court cases, and Otto Ludwig analysed the source of this quality of Kleist's work with remarkable perspicacity: '(Kleist) trägt seine Geschichte vor, wie ein Kriminalist . . . Der Gott bleibt bei ihm in den Wolken, und dadurch entsteht sein Tragisches; dies ist bei ihm eben, dass die Menschen leiden und

---

[1] A. Wilbrandt: *Heinrich von Kleist*, 1863, p. 155.
[2] This technique is particularly noticeable in *Penthesilea* and *Prinz Friedrich von Homburg*. Cf. J. Petersen, loc. cit., p. 355, P. Kluckhohn: *Die deutsche Romantik* 1924, p. 256 passim, B. Schulze: *Das Bild als Leitmotiv in den Dramen Kleists und anderer Dichter, Zeitschrift für deutschen Unterricht*, Vol. XXIV, p. 308 passim, O. Walzel: *Leitmotive in Dichtungen, Zeitschrift für Bücherfreunde*, Vol. VIII, p. 10, and F. Servaes: *H. v. Kleist*, 1902, p. 50 ff.
[3] Cf. C. Lugowski: *Wirklichkeit und Dichtung*, 1936, p. 138.

handeln, sie wissen nicht warum und wozu.'[1] [xliv]. This form implies the construction of a continuous series of scenes, rather than a balanced division into Acts. While Kleist used the latter technique in the majority of his plays, the composition of a continuous action was more suited to his genius. From the technical point of view he produced his best work in this manner, e.g., in *Der Zerbrochene Krug* and *Penthesilea*, although there is, as we shall see, reason to doubt the validity of this view in the case of the latter drama. The form of Kleist's plays, moreover, is characterized by the position of the climax. In his tragedies it is not placed where it is found in classical drama, viz. in the third Act, but much nearer the end, so that the climax and the catastrophe tend to coincide in his work. For this purpose, again, an uninterrupted series of scenes was the most suitable form. If we judge Kleist's dramas by classical standards, they will be found deficient in the use of the dénouement and lacking in the qualities of balance and symmetry. But in applying these standards we expose ourselves to the danger of misinterpreting the formal values of his work.

Another feature of Kleist's technique is revealed in his lack of attention to the material aspect of the dramatic plot. The physical events remain in the background of the action and our interest is primarily aroused by the spiritual condition of the characters and the emotional relations between them. Kleist frequently used a device, well-known in Greek and French tragedy, by which important incidents are not directly represented on the stage, but are given in commentaries of eye-witnesses or in reports by messengers. This technique, most tellingly used in the battle-scenes of *Penthesilea* and *Prinz Friedrich von Homburg*, permitted Kleist to work out fully the emotional value of the incidents and to display the effect which they have on the characters to whom they are reported by the narrators. 'Nicht das' he wrote in a letter dated Chalons-sur-Marne, June 1807 'was dem Sinn dargestellt ist, sondern das, was das Gemüt durch diese Wahrnehmung erregt, ist das Kunstwerk.' [xlv]. He emphasized emotional states of mind resulting from events, rather than the events themselves, and for this reason the two features of his technique, the musical design and the dialectic structure, are equally important aspects of his dramatic compositions and they usually, if not always, combine to produce an impression of consistent unity.

Both Schiller and Kleist declared that it was their desire to produce

[1] *Shakespeare Studien*, ed. Heydrich, 1874, p. 347.

synthesis of Classical and Shakespearean drama. The significance of Kleist's aim will become apparent when we examine his *Robert Guiskard*. Considering it as a problem of form we can say that his project was not to fuse the bustling physical activity of some of Shakespeare's plays (to which the dramatists of the 'Sturm und Drang' had been principally attracted) with the static effects of Greek tragedy, but to combine, if he could, the psychological depth of the one with the formal perfection of the other. The synthesis of musical and dialectic elements supplied him with the means to achieve this end.

'In der Kunst' he wrote in a letter to Collin on February 14, 1808, 'kommt es überall auf die Form an, und Alles was eine Gestalt hat, ist meine Sache'. [xlvi]. It is significant that he said this, for his dramas, judged by traditional standards, may be held to lack perfection of form. When the musical quality of his technique is appreciated, however, the truth of his statement becomes clear, as well as the meaning of the following passage from his *Brief eines Dichters an einen anderen*:

Sprache, Rhythmus, Wohlklang u.s.w., so reizend diese Dinge auch, insofern sie den Geist einhüllen, sein mögen, so sind sie doch an und für sich ... nichts, als ein wahrer, obschon natürlicher und notwendiger Übelstand; und die Kunst kann, in bezug auf sie, auf nichts gehen, als sie möglichst verschwinden zu machen. Ich bemühe mich aus meinen besten Kräften, dem Ausdruck Klarheit, dem Versbau Bedeutung, dem Klang der Worte Anmut und Leben zu geben: aber bloss, damit diese Dinge gar nicht, vielmehr einzig und allein der Gedanke, den sie einschliessen, erscheine. Denn das ist die Eigenschaft aller echten Form, dass der Geist augenblicklich und unmittelbar daraus hervortritt, während die mangelhafte ihn, wie ein schlechter Spiegel, gebunden hält, und uns an nichts erinnert, als an sich selbst. [xlvii].

This pronouncement is the antithesis of Schiller's statement: 'In einem wahrhaft schönen Kunstwerk soll der Inhalt nichts, die Form aber alles tun'[1] [xlviii] but it does not imply that Kleist depreciated the value of form as such. He only rejected a particular kind of form, the form which is dictated by absolute standards of beauty and which is imposed upon any material, regardless of its quality. Against the practice of the Weimar Classicists he revived Herder's ideas of the expressive style, of 'characteristic art', at a time when Goethe and

[1] *Briefe über die ästhetische Erziehung des Menschen*, Letter 22. *Werke, Säkularausgabe*, Vol. XII, p. 85.

Schiller, who had spoken for it in their youth, denied its aesthetic value.[1]

Kleist's principal consideration in fashioning his style was expressiveness. To this end he sacrificed the values which were of supreme importance for other poets—the enchanting epithet, the mellifluous phrase, the happy cadence—and he eschewed all forms of embellishment for its own sake. His desire to elaborate a characteristic rather than a beautiful mode of expression and his passion for absolute veracity are revealed in the laborious corrections which he made in his manuscripts before submitting them for publication. It has been shown that the principles which guided him in making these alterations are explained by his desire to be expressive regardless of other considerations, e.g. the repetition of certain phrases for the sake of emphasis, the use of telling adjectives, the addition of dynamic, not necessarily embellishing or euphonious verbs, prepositions and interjections, the substitution of similes and metaphors for earlier vaguer formulations, the accumulative use of images, the sacrifice of regular metres and the concentration on rhythmical rather than metrical patterns.[2] In the interest of expressiveness, too, he made extensive use of rhetorical pauses and retardations in the action and in the speech of his characters. He explained his methods in the essay *Über die allmähliche Verfertigung der Gedanken beim Reden* (1806): 'Ich mische unartikulierte Töne ein, ziehe die Verbindungswörter in die Länge, gebrauche auch wohl eine Apposition, wo sie nicht nötig wäre, und bediene mich anderer, die Rede ausdehnender, Kunstgriffe, zur Fabrikation meiner Idee auf der Werkstätte der Vernunft, die gehörige Zeit zu gewinnen.' [xlix].

Kleist's passionate desire to be truthful also accounts for the naturalistic elements in his work. Just as he did not conform to the view that it is the purpose of the tragedian's art to temper the emotions, but set out to give them the greatest intensity, so also he was impelled by the aim to express with utmost veracity and cogency and without suppression or modification, the thoughts and feelings within him. In a letter, dated August 1811, he wrote: 'Alsdann will ich meinem Herzen ganz und gar, wo es mich hinführt, folgen, und schlechterdings auf nichts Rücksicht nehmen, als auf meine eigene innerliche Befriedigung . . . Kurz, ich will mich von dem Gedanken ganz durchdringen, dass, wenn ein Werk nur recht frei aus dem

---

[1] Cf. Goethe's essay on the Strassburg Cathedral as against the later *Der Sammler und die Seinigen* as well as Schiller's *Vom Gemeinen und Niedrigen in der Kunst*.
[2] Cf. T. Kaiser: loc. cit., esp. pp. 102–276.

Schoss des menschlichen Gemüts hervorgeht, dasselbe auch notwendig darum der ganzen Menschheit angehören müsse.'[l]. If the bent of his imagination, the dialectic of his inward impulses dictated to him,. he would make no concessions to convention or good taste and he would not stop at the presentation of even the most gruesome emotions and cruel actions. There was undoubtedly a strain of cruelty in his nature. He expressed it by making some of his characters (e.g. Jupiter, Wetter vom Strahl, Hermann, the Kurfürst) teasingly, even sadistically, torture those who are really near and dear to them. Similarly, moral considerations were of secondary importance for him in aesthetic matters and he blamed the taste of women for the wide popularity enjoyed in his day by Iffland and Kotzebue: 'Wenn man es recht untersucht, so sind zuletzt die Frauen an dem ganzen Verfall unserer Bühne Schuld, und sie sollten entweder gar nicht ins Schauspiel gehen, oder es müssten eigene Bühnen für sie, abgesondert von den Männern, errichtet werden. Ihre Anforderungen an Sittlichkeit und Moral vernichten das ganze Wesen des Drama'. [li].

Kleist's work offers a striking contrast not only with the popular drama of his day, but also with that of Goethe and Schiller and it is hardly surprising that Goethe, although he accepted some of his plays for performance on the Weimar stage, regarded Kleist, the dramatist and the man, with 'Schauder und Abscheu.'[1]

5

In his essay *Über die allmähliche Verfertigung der Gedanken beim Reden* Kleist propounded an interesting theory. He believed that there are two methods of expressing ideas, one of finding suitable words for an idea that had been thought out beforehand, the other of finding the idea in the act of speaking, i.e. of expressing nascent thought. 'Der Franzose sagt' he wrote 'l'appétit vient en mangeant, und dieser Erfahrungssatz bleibt wahr, wenn man ihn parodiert, und sagt, l'idée vient en parlant.' [liii]. A confused expression, he maintained, does not necessarily indicate confused thinking: 'Wenn daher eine Vorstellung verworren ausgedrückt wird, so folgt der Schluss noch gar nicht, dass sie auch verworren gedacht worden sei'. [liv]. He quotes instances where embarrassment was the cause of faulty expres-

[1] *Ludwig Tiecks Dramaturgische Blätter.* Cf. Goethe's statement in a conversation about Kleist: 'Goethe tadelt an ihm die nordische Schärfe des Hypochonders; es sei einem gereiften Verstande unmöglich, in die Gewaltsamkeit solcher Motive, wie er sich ihrer als Dichter bediene, mit Vergnügen einzugehen . . . Es gäbe ein Unschönes in der Natur, ein Beängstigendes, mit dem sich die Dichtkunst bei noch so kunstreicher Behandlung weder befassen, noch aussöhnen könne' (Biedermann *Goethes Gespräche*, Vol. II, p. 106). [lii].

sion and arrives at the provocative conclusion: 'Nicht wir wissen, es ist allererst ein gewisser Zustand unsrer, welcher weiss.' [lv].

Kleist has described his own method of composition in this essay. He did not work out his plots carefully before proceeding to elaborate them in detail, as Schiller and Lessing usually did. After receiving the initial impetus, Kleist allowed himself to be carried along by the current of his imagination. Hence there are many unexpected developments in his dramas, many apparent inconsistencies and incongruities. He did not always succeed in expressing his ideas, although he may have known what he wanted to say. The ideas may have been definite enough, but they remained at the back of his mind, because he was not capable of expressing them fully. Such an idea is his conception of God. Despite his passion for veracity and his resolution to follow the voice of his heart 'ganz und gar, wo es mich hinführt,' he had his inhibitions. To say outright what he secretly thought would have conflicted with his 'inward satisfaction'. It is difficult to escape the impression that in his pessimistic period Kleist identified God with Fate or Chance, those features of life that filled him with the deepest despair. But neither in his letters nor in his dramas does he explicitly formulate this identification, and yet only when we assume that it, in fact, existed in his own mind, do his tragedies make sense.[1] Viewing together *Die Familie Schroffenstein*, *Amphitryon* and *Penthesilea* we arrive at the conclusion that the ultimate, if unacknowledged source of his pessimism, and thus the core of the motivation in his tragedies, is his conception of the attitude of God to man. An examination of these plays will show that in them God, or else the representative of the divine power (Jupiter in *Amphitryon*, Mars in *Penthesilea*) is either indifferent to human suffering, or intervenes in human affairs to produce suffering, without bodily appearing in the latter play.

However, in *Penthesilea*, Kleist does not use this theme for the motivation of the whole tragedy as he did in earlier dramas, and indeed after completing this work he abandoned the writing of tragedies. His last three plays exhibit a more hopeful attitude to life. He never achieved a stable relationship with his fellow-men, but his distrust of human nature and of the powers that rule man's existence became less pronounced and gave way to a more optimistic outlook. There is, accordingly, a change in his treatment of the themes that he had dealt with in his tragedies. These themes do not disappear entirely

[1] Cf. M. Prigge-Kruhoeffer: *H. v. Kleist, Religiosität und Charakter, Jahrbuch der Kleist Gesellschaft* 1923–1924, esp. p. 46 *passim*.

from his work, but they were given a new direction and they express a new purpose.

In his last plays, however, Kleist does not so much solve the tragic problems of his earlier dramas, as override them. Kant's philosophy had thrown him into despair. Now he has found a way out, but his new creed is not a logical answer to his earlier doubts. The grounds of his optimism cannot be correlated with the reasons for his pessimism. He had written to Wilhelmine von Zenge on March 28, 1801: 'Der Irrtum liegt nicht im Herzen, er liegt im Verstande und nur der Verstand kann ihn heben'. [lvi]. He did not obey his own principle. Against his earlier fears there now stand his hopes. The outlook of the later dramas is simply the reversal of that displayed in the tragedies, and although Kleist's work as a whole possesses unity, it does not possess the logical unity of Schiller's work or the organic unity of Goethe's.

Nor do the elements of his later belief form a consistent whole. The positive attitude to life revealed in *Käthchen von Heilbronn* is different from that displayed in *Die Hermannsschlacht* and both differ from *Prinz Friedrich von Homburg*. In the first play we observe a new attitude to the problem of the relation of God to man, hence a new estimate of human relationships, in the second drama Kleist's patriotic beliefs are expressed, in the last work we have a portrayal of human relationships without reference to the overruling problem of the nature of God and man. As a drama *Prinz Friedrich von Homburg* is Kleist's most satisfying production because before writing it his metaphysical questionings have patently come to rest. *Die Hermannsschlacht*, too, is a product of his purely human interests, but its dramatic values are inferior to those of his last play. *Käthchen von Heilbronn*, aesthetically not altogether one of Kleist's greatest achievements, is yet a significant work, since it reveals most clearly the change from pessimism to optimism so characteristic of Kleist's mature outlook. Just as the origins of his pessimism are laid bare in his study of Kant and a knowledge of this source facilitates the understanding of his tragedies, so one basis of his optimism can be uncovered and will assist us in the interpretation of his last plays.

When he was in Dresden in 1807, Kleist attended Schubert's lectures on *Ansichten von der Nachtseite der Naturwissenschaften*. Some of the theories put forward by Schubert confirmed him in his efforts to overcome his metaphysical pessimism. On August 31, 1806 he had written to his friend Rühle von Lilienstern: 'Es kann kein böser Geist sein, der an der Spitze der Welt steht, es ist ein bloss unbegriffe-

c

ner !' [lvii]. In this letter there is no trace of his former despair. At that time he was composing his *Penthesilea* and the ambiguities contained in this work can only be explained if we assume that he was changing his views about the relation of God and man at the time when he was writing the play. This tragedy reveals elements of his new faith, while it also exhibits features of his earlier dramas.

Kleist has himself emphasized the close relationship between *Penthesilea* and his next work, *Käthchen von Heilbronn*. He described the heroine of the latter work as the 'obverse of Penthesilea' and wrote, in a letter to Collin on December 8, 1808: 'Denn wer das Käthchen liebt, dem kann die Penthesilea nicht ganz unbegreiflich sein, sie gehören ja wie das + und das — der Algebra zusammen, und sind Ein und dasselbe Wesen, nur unter entgegengesetzten Beziehungen gedacht.' [lviii]. His revaluation of life, which is so strikingly manifested in *Käthchen* began in 1807 when he composed *Penthesilea*.

The letter to Rühle, written in that year, hints at the new direction of his thought. 'Jede erste Bewegung' Kleist says 'alles Unwillkürliche ist schön; und schief und verschroben Alles, so bald es sich selbst begreift. O der Verstand! Der unglückselige Verstand!' [lix]. The new element that we find in Kleist's thought is contained in the phrase 'alles Unwillkürliche ist schön.' Kleist's distrust of the intellect persists, but now he laments not so much the fact that the mind is incapable of grasping the truth, as the fact that it distorts the beauty of involuntary action. The intellect, too, now represents for him the power of self-comprehension, not, as earlier, the faculty directed towards the understanding of external reality. Clearly, Kleist is under the influence of a new set of philosophical propositions. They are, to a large extent, of his own making, but he also appears to have derived much benefit from his association with Romantic writers, notably with Adam Müller and Schubert.

It would be an over-simplification to call Kleist's thought in his later work 'Romantic'. Just as he had developed his own peculiar view of life from a cursory acquaintance with Kant's philosophy, so he conceived his new ideas without adopting the most characteristic theories of the Romantics. But he was also indebted to Adam Müller's lectures on German science, literature and art held in Dresden in 1806, and to Schubert's lectures on the 'night-side of natural science' of the same year. The result of these contacts is seen in Kleist's profound and suggestive essay *Über das Marionettentheater*, as well as in *Käthchen von Heilbronn*. An equally important influence on these works appears to have been Schiller's *Über Anmut und Würde*, although again Kleist's remarkable originality must be emphasized.

In his essay *Über Anmut und Würde* Schiller, while he modified some of Kant's leading ideas, kept well within the limits of the *Kritik der Urteilskraft*. He defined grace as follows:

> Anmut ist eine Schönheit, die nicht von der Natur gegeben, sondern von dem Subjekte selbst hervorgebracht wird . . . Anmut ist die Schönheit der Gestalt unter dem Einfluss der Freiheit; die Schönheit derjenigen Erscheinungen, die die Person bestimmt . . . Grazie ist immer nur die Schönheit der durch Freiheit bewegten Gestalt, und Bewegungen, die bloss der Natur angehören, können nie diesen Namen verdienen. [lx].[1]

Schiller emphasized the moral freedom of a person in an attitude or an action that he called graceful. He also recognized that such an attitude or action must be involuntary, but he insisted that the source of true Grace lay in the realm of moral freedom: 'Eine willkürliche Bewegung, wenn sie sich nicht . . . mit etwas Unwillkürlichem, das in dem moralischen Empfindungszustand der Person seinen Grund hat, vermischet, kann niemals Grazie zeigen, wozu immer ein Zustand im Gemüt als Ursache erfordert wird'. [lxi][2]

A similar definition—in terms of pre-Kantian terminology, however—is found in Winckelmann's essay *Von der Grazie in Werken der Kunst*:

> Die Grazie ist das vernünftig Gefällige . . . Sie bildet sich durch Erziehung und Überlegung und kann zur Natur werden, welche dazu geschaffen ist. Sie ist ferne vom Zwange und gesuchten Witze, aber es erfordert Aufmerksamkeit und Fleiss, die Natur in allen Handlungen, wo sie sich nach eines jeden Talent zu zeigen hat, auf den rechten Grad der Leichtigkeit zu erheben. In der Einfalt und in der Stille der Seele wirkt sie und wird durch ein wildes Feuer und in aufgebrachten Neigungen verdunkelt. [lxii].[3]

Both Schiller and Winckelmann saw the true expression of grace in the living human figure or its artistic representation. In his essay *Über das Marionettentheater*, Kleist puts forward the view that the puppet possesses this quality in the highest degree and that 'es dem Menschen schlechthin unmöglich wäre, den Gliedermann darin auch nur zu erreichen.' [lxiii]. The puppet, he says, is infinitely graceful because it has no will of its own, since it is completely obedient to the superior will that rules it, and because it is 'antigrav', i.e. because it is not tied to earth by the force of gravity —

---

[1] *Werke, Säkularausgabe*, Vol. XI, pp. 185, 195 f.   [2] Ibid., p. 198 f.   [3] Loc. cit., p. 155 f.

'weil die Kraft, die sie in die Lüfte erhebt, grösser ist, als jene, die sie an die Erde fesselt.' [lxiv]. Man's nature is the antithesis of that of the marionette; his body is ruled by the law of gravity and his will obstructs the higher will, the will of God. After reference has been made to the third chapter of the Book of Genesis, Kleist continues: 'Ich sagte, dass ich gar wohl wüsste, welche Unordnungen, in der natürlichen Grazie des Menschen, das Bewusstsein anrichtet'. [lxv]. It is the mind of man, his knowledge and his will, that disturb the beauty and harmony of his being: 'Wir sehen, dass in dem Masse, als, in der organischen Welt, die Reflexion dunkler und schwächer wird, die Grazie darin immer strahlender und herrschender hervortritt.' [lxvi].

The faculty that produces the highest form of grace for Schiller is just that which obstructs it for Kleist. Since human knowledge, Kleist believed, was imperfect, it disturbed the harmony of man's being, so that, if the integrity of man's character is to be restored, the human race must progress to the achievement of the only true knowledge, which is that of God, or rule it out entirely and so attain to the state of the puppet: 'So findet sich auch, wenn die Erkenntnis gleichsam durch ein Unendliches gegangen ist, die Grazie wieder ein; so, dass sie, zu gleicher Zeit, in demjenigen menschlichen Körperbau am reinstèn erscheint, der entweder gar keins, oder ein unendliches Bewusstsein hat, d.h. in dem Gliedermann, oder in dem Gott. — Mithin, sagte ich ein wenig zerstreut, müssten wir wieder von dem Baum der Erkenntnis essen, um in den Stand der Unschuld zurückzufallen? — Allerdings, antwortete er, das ist das letzte Kapitel von der Geschichte der Welt.' [lxvii].

This suggestive conversation, so remarkable for its light and almost ironic treatment of the most profound ideas, gives a good indication of the new direction of Kleist's thought. It reveals that his ideal is now not sublimity, but beauty. The acceptance of the ideal of beauty and of grace presumes a belief in universal harmony and with Kleist it suggests a return to the creed of his youth, the belief in a benevolent Deity ruling the life of man. After completing his tragedies he arrived at the conclusion, as Schiller did, that the highest aim of the dramatist could be achieved 'wenn selbst diese Unzufriedenheit mit dem Schicksal hinwegfällt und sich in die Ahnung oder lieber in ein deutliches Bewusstsein einer teleologischen Verknüpfung der Dinge, einer erhabenen Ordnung, eines gütigen Willens verliert.' [lxviii].[1] Upon the basis of a similar belief Kleist constructed his drama *Käthchen von Heilbronn*.

[1] *Über die tragische Kunst, Werke, Säkularausgabe*, Vol. XI, p. 165.

While Wetter vom Strahl possesses a will of his own and thus obstructs the divine will, Käthchen is a puppet without 'Bewusstsein'. The only character in Kleist's earlier dramas with whom we can compare her in this respect is Agnes in *Die Familie Schroffenstein*, whose trust in the goodness of human beings gives her the beauty that Käthchen possesses by virtue of her naïveté.[1] The difference between Kleist's earlier and his later works lies in the fact that Agnes becomes a tragic victim of circumstances, while Käthchen achieves happiness. The ultimate reason for this difference is the effective intervention of God in the lives of the principal characters, whereas in *Die Familie Schroffenstein* God is silent and even appears to will the tragic catastrophe. Kleist's reassessment of values is seen in his revaluation of the relation between God and man.

When Kleist wrote *Käthchen von Heilbronn* he had also revised his views on human nature. He was no longer obsessed with the frailty of the human intellect and the tragedy of human error. A treatment of these themes is still to be found in the drama, but they do not dominate the mind of the author as they had done in the tragedies, and even in the comedy *Der Zerbrochene Krug*. The insistence on human error is now overshadowed by the proof of human strength and certainty. The mind of Wetter vom Strahl is incapable of solving the riddles besetting the characters in this play, but Käthchen's instinct is a safe guide towards happiness. When Kleist wrote his tragedies, he regarded both reason and passion as unreliable faculties. Now he emphasized that man's instinct was unerring and infallible. This is the point where he agreed with the Romantics, above all with Novalis, who had said: 'Mit Instinkt hat der Mensch angefangen, mit Instinkt soll der Mensch endigen. Instinkt ist das Genie im Paradiese, vor der Periode der Selbstabsonderung (Selbsterkenntnis).' [lxx][2] This statement recalls to mind the argument in *Über das Marionettentheater* and illuminates its meaning.

For this view of the value of instinct Kleist may also have been indebted to Schubert. There has been much discussion of the possible influence of his *Ansichten von der Nachtseite der Naturwissenschaften* on Kleist's later thought, and it has yielded little positive result. It can be said that Schubert's views on somnambulism are unimportant in this connection, since he discussed its pathological nature and treated somnambulists as hypnotic media, aspects which

---

[1] Cf. Schiller in *Über naive und sentimentalische Dichtung, Werke*, Vol. XII, p. 175: 'Aus der naiven Denkart fliesst notwendigerweise auch ein naiver Ausdruck sowohl in Worten als Bewegungen, und er ist das wichtigste Bestandstück der Grazie.' [lxix].

[2] *Fragmente*, ed. Kamnitzer, p. 416.

are not to be found in Kleist's use of the phenomenon in *Käthchen von Heilbronn* and *Prinz Friedrich von Homburg*.[1] It is probable that his knowledge of somnambulism was more immediately personal and that it can be traced to his own experiences and to those of Zschokke, with whom he was associated in Switzerland.

There are other elements in Schubert's work which may have influenced Kleist more strongly and more positively, or, at any rate, may have assisted him in his search for new beliefs. It was Schubert's purpose, in his lectures, to trace 'das älteste Verhältnis des Menschen zu der Natur, die lebendige Harmonie des Einzelnen mit dem Ganzen'. [lxxi]. This view, as we have seen, is the basis of Kleist's revived optimism. Furthermore, Schubert discussed the faculties of instinct and will. The latter, he said, developed later in man than the former, and instinct, he asserted, was a safer guide than the other faculty: 'Wir finden selten, dass der natürliche Trieb Täuschungen oder Missgriffen ausgesetzt sei, wohl aber ist dieses in gewisser Hinsicht der Wille'.[2] [lxxii] From the testimony of the *Marionettentheater* and of *Käthchen von Heilbronn* we are able to conclude that it was this aspect of Schubert's work which Kleist absorbed, that it was linked in his mind with the conception of a benevolent Deity and that by means of a fusion of these ideas he was able to overcome the pessimism of his youth.

The fundamental unity of Kleist's work, however, is revealed by the fact that this valuation of instinct does not appear for the first time in his later work. It is an essential feature of his tragic representations no less than the cardinal principle of his romantic drama. In his earlier plays it may be discovered in his assessment of 'Gefühl' which signified for him the possession of a profound inward certainty— a faculty as different from passion as it is from the intellect. 'Folge nie,' he wrote in a letter dated January 11–12, 1801, 'dem dunklen Triebe (i.e. passion), der immer zu dem Gemeinen führt . . . Was dein erstes Gefühl Dir antwortet, das tue.' [lxxiii]. In another letter (January 31, 1801) he wrote: 'Immer nannte er (Brockes) den Verstand kalt und nur das Herz wirkend und schaffend . . . Immer seiner ersten Regung gab er sich ganz hin, das nannte er seinen Gefühlsblick, und ich selbst habe nie gefunden, dass dieser ihn getäuscht habe.' [lxxiv]. Fundamentally this feeling is the instinctive knowledge

---

[1] Cf. A. Béguin's view: 'On n'a pas manqué d'évoquer l'influence de Schubert . . . Mais il faut être prudent dans ces rapprochements . . . toutes les intentions de son (Kleist's) art donnent, aux matériaux romantiques, une inflexion très particulière' (*L'Ame Romantique et le Rêve*, 1937, Vol. II, p. 305).

[2] *Ansichten von der Nachtseite der Naturwissenschaft*, 1808, p. 28.

of what is right and proper, a 'Rechtsgefühl' as Kleist uses this term. It appears in those of Kleist's characters who reveal the positive aspects of his belief—in Eustache, Sylvester, Agnes and Alkmene. This feeling may become confused, but it suffers confusion only when passion triumphs over it (as in Sylvester) or when the appearances of external reality prove overwhelming (as in Alkmene). In itself it is for Kleist, in his tragic period, the only source of truth. His tragedies depict the contamination of this source by the intervention of a malicious power and by the triumph of suspicion and hatred over love. In *Kätchen von Heilbronn*, on the other hand, the source remains pure because it is protected by a benevolent Deity.

Kleist's fundamentally critical temperament, however, did not allow him to base his philosophy of life permanently on the acceptance of a belief in the miraculous order of things. A more stable affirmation of the values of life is found only in *Prinz Friedrich von Homburg*, where the problem is no longer the relation between God and man, but that between the individual and the state. Here, too, Kleist gives an original presentation of the problem and its solution and neither Adam Müller nor any other thinker of the Romantic era supplied him with ideas or formulae. In this drama, as in his other work, it is Kleist's 'innerstes Wesen' that is the true source of his inspiration. 'Es ist wahr, mein innerstes Wesen liegt darin' [lxxv] he said this about the tragedy *Penthesilea* in a letter written during 1807 and the same is true of his last play. Here Kleist reveals an astonishing sense of balance, in his psychological emphases as well as in his use of formal values. The metaphysical disorders of his youth reverberate only as faint echoes and the fanciful constructions of *Käthchen von Heilbronn* have been put aside. Those 'romantic' fancies had their educative value for Kleist, for, once achieved they made all further speculation on the subject of the ultimate nature of life unnecessary. Kleist was free to consider life in its practical issues, which the Napoleonic Wars made imperative. This task he performed savagely in *Die Hermannsschlacht* and nobly in *Prinz Friedrich von Homburg*. These two plays, whatever the differences between their moral and their artistic values may be, represent the culmination of Kleist's achievement, the resolution of his life's disharmonies.

ROBERT GUISKARD and DIE FAMILIE SCHROFFENSTEIN

FOR an appreciation of Kleist's tragedies and of his development as a dramatist, it is of some importance to consider whether *Robert Guiskard* or *Die Familie Schroffenstein* is his first work. Because of Kleist's reticence concerning the composition of his plays, we are not in a position to decide with complete certainty in what order they were written. We know that the first drafts of both *Robert Guiskard* and *Die Familie Schroffenstein* were made in Paris during the autumn of 1801. The latter work was completed in 1802 and appeared in print in the following year, while the former had probably reached a somewhat greater degree of maturity in Paris than *Die Familie Schroffenstein*. Dissatisfied with his work Kleist destroyed the manuscript of *Robert Guiskard*, but later he re-wrote the first scenes and published them as a fragment in the journal *Phöbus* in 1808.

Although the fragment was composed at approximately the same time as *Penthesilea* and reveals many similarities with this work in points of syntax, imagery and vocabulary, essentially it belongs to Kleist's earliest period. There is no justification for assuming that he altered the content of his tragedy when he published the fragment. Even the material contained in the opening ten scenes, slender though it is, suffices to substantiate the view that he followed his original project in the *Phöbus*-text and that this project was based on an idea of tragedy very different from that which underlies *Die Familie Schroffenstein*. There is a clear line of development from this latter drama to *Amphitryon* and to *Penthesilea*. Here the tragic problems were determined by Kleist's views of life which resulted from his interpretation of Kant's philosophy. Each of these dramas gives a presentation of human behaviour in circumstances for which the human beings principally concerned in the dramatic action are not primarily responsible. The dramatic interest lies chiefly in the excess of passion and in the errors of judgment which these characters reveal when faced with such a set of circumstances.

As far as we are able to judge, the dramatic problem in *Robert Guiskard* is of another kind. There appear to be three main centres of interest in this work: Guiskard himself, his army, and the members of his family. Undoubtedly Guiskard was to occupy a dominating position in the dramatic action; the fortunes of his family and of his army were to be of secondary importance compared with his own. Nevertheless, the army and the family were not a mere background of the tragic action, they were an essential part of it. This is shown by the vivid and emphatic description of the army surging around Guiskard's tent like the tempestuous sea around a rock, and by the clear-cut characterization of such figures as the old warrior, Abälard and Guiskard's son Robert. The ten scenes are filled with diversified dramatic life, revealing first the sufferings of the plague-stricken army, then the rivalry between Abälard and the younger Robert and finally Guiskard's attempt to conceal from his soldiers the manifest truth that he has himself become a victim of the plague. The central conflict of the drama is revealed in the tenth scene. Guiskard, impelled by his ambition to capture the beleaguered city of Constantinople, is halted by the outbreak of the disease at the moment when he learns that the city will yield to him only if he will himself assume the Imperial Byzantine Crown. Probably the drama was to present Guiskard's heroic resistance to the dangers besetting him and his final defeat by the plague and by the intrigues of Abälard, the rightful heir to the leadership of the Normans.

If this is the course which the dramatic action was to follow, and the majority of the critics believe that it is, then we can, with our knowledge of Kleist's beginnings as a writer, postulate that this tragedy was his first effort in the field of the drama, preceding even *Die Familie Schroffenstein*. His intellectual experiences, particularly the influence of Kant, are more immediately manifest in this latter work. The political theme underlying *Robert Guiskard*, the importance of ambition as a motive power of the action, and the emphasis upon deceit and intrigue in the working out of the plot, are features characteristic of a traditional form of tragedy, such as are found in Shakespeare and in Schiller's *Wallenstein*, a work which Kleist greatly admired and to which he frequently referred in his letters to Wilhelmine von Zenge. However bold in design and execution, *Robert Guiskard* lacks the originality of *Die Familie Schroffenstein* as regards the conception of the tragic conflict and the characterization of the principal figures. When he chose the theme of *Robert Guiskard*, Kleist was more indebted to purely literary models than in any of his later works. It is clearly the product of a poetic apprenticeship and it was inspired by Kleist's ambition to vie with the greatest authors in their own sphere and, at the same time, his tribute to the supreme examples of dramatic art. Kleist's literary interests rather than his philosophical experiences impelled him to write *Robert Guiskard*, and it is not surprising that the project dissatisfied him. He destroyed the work when he had nearly completed it because the material which he had chosen could not be made to represent the pessimistic view of life which his reading of Kant had led him to adopt. A drama on an heroic scale was not the most suitable medium for expressing his particular feelings, since it was not the rare qualities of human nature, but the fundamental condition of man that inspired his misgivings about life.

Kleist's originality as a dramatist lies in his treatment of the theme of human fallibility. It is the dominant motif of his most characteristic tragedies and it most clearly defines his intellectual position. By treating this theme he was able to escape the necessity of dealing with the question of human responsibility and to imply that the actions of men and women were largely the product of circumstances over which they had no control. This is the situation facing us in Kleist's tragedies from *Die Familie Schroffenstein* to *Penthesilea*. In *Robert Guiskard*, as far as we can judge, the problem of guilt was to play a more important part. Kleist's footnotes in the printed text arouse the feeling that Guiskard, although he possesses the complete confidence of his army, has in fact usurped the position of leadership in the Norman state, and that he is endeavouring to secure the succession of his own son, disregarding the rightful claims of his nephew Abälard. Further, it is hinted that he considers the proposals of the traitors in Constantinople with favour. The situation in *Robert Guiskard* therefore strongly resembles that which Schiller had dramatized in *Wallenstein*, a tragedy with an unmistakable moral tendency. The fragmentary nature of the material prevents us from arriving at any safe conclusions concerning the significance of Guiskard's guilt for the tragic dénouement, but it is clear that his moral responsibility was to form an integral part of the dramatic idea. As in Schiller's tragedy, the hero acts in obedience to the promptings of his personal ambition, is involved in deceit and intrigue and, we may surmise for Kleist's drama, suffers the penalty of defeat.

In another respect *Robert Guiskard* resembles *Wallenstein*, although on this point an important difference between the two works may also be observed, a difference which reveals the contrasting qualities in the dramatic approach of Schiller and Kleist. In both tragedies the ambitious schemes of the hero are thwarted by the intervention

of an outside power, by Fate. Wallenstein's plans are doomed to
failure when his envoy Sesina is captured by his opponents. Guiskard's
efforts are nullified by an outbreak of the plague, to which he himself
succumbs. The difference lies in the quality of the obstructing force.
In Schiller's drama it is part of the human world, it is something that
Wallenstein might have foreseen. The plague is an unpredictable
event, an accident beyond the control of Guiskard. Schiller humanised the power of Fate, in order to clarify the moral problem underlying his drama. Kleist is more radical. In his tragedy Fate is an
irrational force, and human effort is unable to hold it in abeyance.
Wallenstein's guilt and his misfortune are clearly related together as
cause and effect. His misfortune overtakes him because he has gone
too far in his guilt. Kleist's fragment gives us no indications of a
similar concatenation of guilt and Fate. The two motive powers
leading to Guiskard's tragic defeat are parallel but unconnected
elements of the dramatic plot. It may well be that Kleist destroyed the
manuscript of his play because it suffered from this irremediable
inner contradiction, because he had over-emphasized the importance
of Guiskard's guilt and thus obscured his own true feelings about the
power of Fate in the lives of men.

By giving equal weight to his hero's ambition and to the plague,
however, Kleist endeavoured to construct an ideal tragedy, a drama
that combined in itself the essential characteristics of ancient Greek
and of modern, that is to say Shakespearean, tragedy. This view is
borne out by C. M. Wieland's eulogy of Kleist. 'Wenn die Geister
des Aeschylus, Sophokles und Shakespeares' he wrote[1] 'sich vereinig-
ten, eine Tragödie zu schaffen, sie würde das sein, was Kleists Tod
Guiskards des Normannen, sofern das Ganze demjenigen entspräche,
was er mich damals hören liess. Von diesem Augenblick an war es
bei mir entschieden, Kleist sei dazu geboren, die grosse Lücke in
unserer dramatischen Literatur auszufüllen, die, nach meiner Meinung
wenigstens, selbst von Schiller und Goethe nicht ausgefüllt worden
ist.' [xxvi]. When Wieland wrote these profoundly uncritical words,
he could not have known more of Kleist's work than the published
Schroffenstein and an oral account of, or reading from, *Robert Guiskard*.
We may even doubt whether he knew the former drama, if he meant
his words to be taken seriously. It was, perhaps, more Kleist's promise
than his performance that inspired Wieland's eulogy and it is probable
that Kleist himself conveyed to Wieland his intention to create a
drama that represented a fusion of Greek and Shakespearean elements

[1] In a letter dated April 10, 1804.

in tragedy—an ideal to which *Die Familie Schroffenstein* does not conform. It is an ideal which was characteristic of Kleist's ambition at the beginning of his literary career, but which he failed to achieve.

Kleist shared the aim of creating such a drama with other writers of his time. Goethe, Schiller and Friedrich Schlegel also endeavoured, each in a different way, to produce a 'synthesis' of ancient and modern tragedy. Ever since Lessing and Herder had examined the qualities of Greek and of Shakespearean drama, the two forms of tragedy had been recognized as equal in value but different in kind. How, then, could the attempt be made to fuse them into an ideal unity? It was based on the view, current among critics in Germany and elsewhere at the end of the eighteenth century, that Greek tragedy was essentially the representation of man in conflict with Fate or Destiny, whereas in Shakespearean tragedy the characters are the authors of their own misfortunes. Sophocles' *Œdipus* was considered the archetype of ancient, *Hamlet* the model of modern, tragedy. In the field of criticism the difficulty of bringing the two forms under a common denominator is revealed in Lessing's endeavour, when he defined the rôle of character in drama, to obey the requirements of Aristotle's theory and at the same time to account for Shakespeare. For the creative dramatist of the eighteenth century the problem resolved itself into the task of preserving the integrity of four elements: Fate as the determinant of human misfortune, the dominating position of the tragic hero, the unity of the dramatic action, and freedom of movement within the tragic economy. Eventually it was found that the aspiration to fuse these elements into a single whole could not be achieved and that the attempt itself was an artificial undertaking. It was based on a one-sided view of the essential qualities of Greek and of Shakespearean tragedy, since the differences between the two forms of the drama are not as fundamental as they were thought to be.

Wieland believed that in *Robert Guiskard* Kleist travelled farther along the path of success than Schiller had done in *Wallenstein* and in *Die Braut von Messina*; this view is justifiable on the grounds that Kleist's conception of Fate was more radical and his attitude to the problem of guilt in drama more amoral than those of Schiller. There is, indeed, a striking resemblance between *Œdipus* and *Robert Guiskard*. In both dramas the plague is used as an instrument to reveal the hero's secret and to bring about his downfall. This device enabled Kleist to adapt the form of Greek tragedy to the requirements of the modern stage with greater success than even Schiller had achieved.

Schiller studied the technique of the Greek dramatists before he began to write *Wallenstein* and followed their example. He adopted the principles of tragic analysis as far as his material allowed him to do so, by compressing the action into a reasonably short space of time, by selecting a restricted locality for the principal scene of his play and by arranging his plot in such a way that the situation prevailing at the beginning of the dramatic action contained all the decisive factors leading to the development of the climax. We know that Kleist devoted some time to the study of Greek drama before he wrote his early tragedies,[1] and the ten scenes contained in the fragmentary *Robert Guiskard* are as brilliant an example of the technique of tragic analysis as may be found in German literature. By opening his dramatic action at the point when Guiskard is doomed to confinement in his tent while the negotiations with the city of Constantinople demand the most energetic activity from him, Kleist succeeded in constructing a situation, which is a worthy imitation of the exposition in Sophocles' *Œdipus*. In his first drama he reveals himself as a master of that method of progressive revelation, of that 'stationäre Prozessform' which was to remain a prominent feature of his dramatic technique.

There are, however, certain aspects of Kleist's art which distinguish his work from that of other dramatists, particularly from his Greek models. The difference between *Œdipus* and *Robert Guiskard* is no less characteristic of Kleist's intentions than the resemblance between them.

Œdipus is ignorant of the crime that he has committed. He is not aware of having done wrong until the secret of his birth and his childhood are explained. The truth is borne in upon him from outside. He stands in the centre of the tragic developments, but he is their passive agent, not their active initiator. Guiskard, on the other hand, is the dynamic centre of the dramatic occurrences. He is not merely a victim of circumstances like Œdipus whose suffering grows in magnitude the more he becomes aware of the real nature of his own past, but a resolute personality who strives to impose his will on those around him and is prepared to prevaricate in order to achieve his ends. The dramatic action of *Œdipus* consists in the process of unravelling the happenings of a distant past. In *Robert Guiskard* the tragic interest lies mainly in the present and the future; the past is important only because it affects the present situation. In *Œdipus*, too, the present

---

[1] On June 18, 1801, he borrowed Part I of *Das tragische Theater der Griechen* by Steinbrüchel from the Dresden library. This volume contains four dramas of Sophocles, including *Œdipus*.

condition of the hero primarily claims our attention, but it is a
condition which is constantly invaded by the past, so that past and
present intertwine to form an indissoluble unity. There are no reliable
indications in the fragment of *Robert Guiskard* which Kleist has left us
that the hero's past history was to affect his present situation to the
same degree of intensity.

The technique of tragic analysis was the most suitable means for
presenting the conditions which prevailed in *Œdipus*. It was not an
equally effective method if every aspect of the dramatic situation
inherent in the plot of *Robert Guiskard* was to be fully exploited.
It is probable, therefore, that Kleist encountered serious difficulties
of a technical kind in the course of composing his work and his failure
to complete it may be partly accounted for by this predicament. In
his first tragedy he endeavoured to fuse divergent elements into a
unity. He attempted to give equal emphasis to Guiskard's character
and to the force of external circumstances, and he tried to present his
material in a form which possesses the highest poetic value, but which
did not allow him to exhaust all the possibilities of the dramatic
situation he had chosen. Furthermore, the material did not lend itself
to a clear exposition of his own attitude to life. The more Kant's
philosophy imprinted itself on his mind, the more he felt the need to
express his growing conviction of the fallibility of human nature.

Die Familie Schroffenstein is the product both of his disappointment
over the failure to complete *Robert Guiskard* and of his philosophical
disillusionment. It is not an entirely successful attempt to present his
profounder misgivings about life. In the construction of the plot and
in the character delineation there are many obscurities and inconsistencies which are a result of Kleist's manner of evolving his ideas during
the process of writing about them. But if this work is not a clear-cut
exposition of the thoughts and feelings which were growing within
him, it is, as regards both content and form, a nearer approach to
personal expression than *Robert Guiskard* had been.

Some evidence of Kleist's search for self-expression in his first
completed tragedy is contained in the changes which he made during
the period when he composed the work. We possess one draft and
two complete versions of the drama and we are thus able to arrive
at certain conclusions about the first conception and the later elaboration of the material.

There are two principal differences between the earliest draft of
the work entitled *Die Familie Thierrez* and the completed drama.

The figures of Jeronimus and Johann are not to be found in this summary of the dramatic action. Kleist added these figures in order to enforce the central theme of his tragedy. The portion of the tragedy that was most fully worked out in *Die Familie Thierrez* was the relationship between the lovers Agnes and Ottokar or, as they were first called, Ignez and Rodrigo. This episode appears to have been the dramatic nucleus of the whole work. Kleist's personal experiences when he was engaged to Wilhelmine von Zenge and his literary predilections, notably his admiration for *Wallenstein* and *Romeo and Juliet*, may have given him the first impetus in writing his drama. In the process, however, of developing the material which was to serve as the framework of the tale of the lovers, his interest was aroused more and more by the enmity of the two families and this gave him an opportunity to express his profound scepticism about human relationships. In *Die Familie Thierrez* the emphasis is mainly on Ignez and Rodrigo, whereas in the second and the third version of the tragedy, in *Die Familie Ghonorez* and in *Die Familie Schroffenstein* it has shifted to the warring families. This change of emphasis was made possible by the introduction of the figure of Johann, who serves to complicate the hitherto straightforward relations between the lovers. In the later versions Juan and Rodrigo (Johann and Ottokar) become rivals. They are both in love with Agnes, so that our sympathy is now divided among the three figures, whereas formerly it had been claimed only by Rodrigo and Ignez. Kleist attempted to diversify the interest still further in the final version by creating two persons (Ursula and her daughter Barnabè) in place of the single woman he had planned in *Die Familie Thierrez* and by hinting at an intimate relationship between Ottokar and Barnabè.[1] Although he did not develop this motif, it was clearly his intention to reduce the importance of the Agnes-Ottokar action which had dominated the plot in the first draft of the tragedy.

The second change which he made in the economy of the drama was still more significant. He now accentuated the conflict between the houses of Rossitz and Warwand and he used this theme to set forth his pessimistic views of the fallibility of human nature, and his sense of the inextricable confusion of right and wrong in the life of man. In this aspect of the drama the influence of his Kantian experience may be observed and here the difference between the treatment of fate and character in *Robert Guiskard* and of the equivalent tragic factors in *Die Familie Schroffenstein* reveal the progress of Kleist's

[1] Cf. *Die Familie Schroffenstein*, Act IV, Scene 3.

development as a dramatist. It is thus seen that progressively from *Die Familie Thierrez* through *Die Familie Ghonorez* to the final version, he freed himself from the encumberment of preconceived literary notions and penetrated to the deeper sources of his own artistic purpose, and although *Die Familie Schroffenstein* still shows the mark of his dramatic apprenticeship and his inability to express himself lucidly on those matters that most forcibly occupied his mind, it is a true product of his dramatic genius.

After writing the first scheme of his tragedy, Kleist introduced a new figure in *Die Familie Ghonorez*, which he retained in *Die Familie Schroffenstein*. In the former version this character is called Antonio and in the latter Jeronimus. The dramatic function of this person is to act as an ineffectual intermediary between the heads of the two families. He strongly influences the relations of Rupert and Sylvester, and his death in Rossitz provokes the final catastrophe by compelling Sylvester to abandon his conciliatory efforts and so to become embroiled in violence. Just as the invention of Johann provided Kleist with a means to moderate the intensity of the love-episode, so the creation of the character of Jeronimus enabled him to underline the main theme of the drama. The death of Jeronimus and Johann's madness illustrate the course of the tragic events by revealing its inevitable nature, and by demonstrating the perplexity of human life.

When Kleist elaborated his dramatic material after having made the preliminary sketch of its contents, he paid particular attention to this quality of tragic inevitability. In *Die Familie Thierrez* he envisaged a meeting between the heads of the two houses: '(Alonzo) beschwört den Fernando um Frieden. Umsonst'. [lxxvii]. Although Sylvester endeavours to bring about such a meeting in *Die Familie Schroffenstein* and first resolves to go to Rossitz himself, but later consents to allow Jeronimus to speak for him, his efforts come to naught and they even complicate the tragic issue leading to the final catastrophe. He cannot extricate himself from the tangle of errors and misconstructions, and indeed the circumstances surrounding the death of Peter are so mysterious that the tragic end when each of the fathers mistakenly kills his own child, possesses every appearance of ineluctability.

Kleist's endeavour to accentuate the impression of inexorable necessity in his drama is also revealed in three marginal notes contained in the manuscript of the first complete version *Die Familie Ghonorez*: 'Das Schicksal ist ein Taschenspieler — Sturm der Leidenschaft, Raub des Irrtums, Grimm — hat uns zum Narren' (Act I) 'Man könnte eine Hexe aufführen, die wirklich das Schicksal gelenkt hätte' 'Ursula muss zuletzt, ihr Kind suchend, als Schicksalsleiterin auftreten' (Act IV). [lxxviii]. It has been conjectured that these notes were not written by Kleist himself, but were inserted by one of his friends to whom he entrusted the manuscript. For this conjecture, however, there is no evidence, and unless the last words of the final version:

> Geh, alte Hexe, geh. Du spielst gut aus der Tasche,
> Ich bin zufrieden mit dem Kunststück. Geh. [lxxix].

can be attributed to another hand, Kleist must be assumed to have been the author of the marginal notes. Their importance lies in the fact that they indicate his preoccupation with the theme of fate during the period when he was preparing the composition of the last version of the drama, *Die Familie Schroffenstein*.

It is therefore important to consider to what extent the drama became a Fate-tragedy when Kleist completed his final revision. The work is often taken to be a 'Schicksalstragödie' of the type that flourished in Germany from the end of the eighteenth to the second decade of the nineteenth century. Even a cursory examination of Kleist's drama will show that this interpretation is untenable.

Jakob Minor has given a descriptive definition of this type of tragedy based upon the work of the most representative writers of the genre.[1] It is, he says, a tragedy in which fate is not an abstract, but a personified power, determining the events and the outcome of the drama by means of oracles, legends, dreams and similar devices. In this type of tragedy God is represented as an avenging power, visiting the sins of the ancestors upon their distant descendants. Kleist's *Die Familie Schroffenstein* does not contain such a conception of fate. In his drama it is not a 'personified power'. Whatever his intentions may have been after he had completed *Die Familie Ghonorez*, Ursula is not a witch. She is a woman of the most ordinary kind, a 'grave-digger's widow', who practises magic of the commonest order. Although her removal of Peter's finger for superstitious reasons precipitates the dramatic action, she appears on the scene with the finger only when the action has reached its tragic close, and she has no decisive influence on the course of the drama as a whole. She makes the impression of knowing more than she does and of being more influential than she really is. Her final

---

[1] J. Minor: *Zur Geschichte der deutschen Schicksalstragödie und zu Grillparzers Ahnfrau*, Jahrbuch der Grillparzergesellschaft, Vol. IX, p. 64.

D

appearance is not consistent with the part she plays in the previous action.

Nor are the events and the developments in Kleist's tragedy predetermined in the real meaning of this word. The feeling of inevitability which Kleist was at pains to evoke is produced more by the characters of the drama than by the events. Although there are many coincidences affecting the lives of the characters, the dramatic interest lies not in the situations but in the reactions of the characters to them, in the moral dispositions of the men and women involved in these situations. The ultimate source of the tragedy is not to be found in the external world, but in human nature, in the weakness of the characters. In one sense they are themselves responsible for the calamities that befall them.

Yet, when the question is raised whether they are morally guilty or blameless, it is impossible to give a precise answer. Kleist wrote his drama in a mood of intellectual confusion, and although the theme and the treatment are on the whole quite comprehensible and convincing, we are left in a state of perplexity when we consider the deeper issues contained in the work. The world of *Die Familie Schroffenstein* is a thoroughly humanised, an almost mundane, world. Kleist eschewed all effects of a supernatural order. There are no curses and oracles, no dreams and no legends such as those that determine the action of the 'Schicksalstragödie' proper. Nevertheless, the men and women of *Die Familie Schroffenstein* appear to be in the grip of some evil power working within them which prevents the timely discovery of the secret confronting them and forces them ever deeper into guilt and degradation.

This power does not make its presence felt directly, but some of the characters in the drama are not unaware of it. Sylvester's apparently irrelevant reply to his wife's suggestions concerning the death of Jeronimus express his realization of the existence of this destructive force:

> *Gertrude*   Wenn
> Ich wüsste, wie du jetzt gestimmt, viel hätt' ich
> Zu sagen dir.
> *Sylvester*   Es ist ein trüber Tag
> Mit Wind und Regen, viel Bewegung draussen. —
> Es zieht ein unsichtbarer Geist gewaltig
> Nach Einer Richtung alles fort, den Staub,
> Die Wolken und die Wellen. —

Gertrude   Willst du mich,
Sylvester, hören?
Sylvester   Sehr beschäftigt mich
Dort jener Segel — siehst du ihn? Er schwankt
Gefährlich, übel ist sein Stand, er kann
Das Ufer nicht erreichen. —
Gertrude   Höre mich,
Sylvester, eine Nachricht hab' ich dir
Zu sagen von Jerome.
Sylvester   Er, er ist
Hinüber — (Er wendet sich) ich weiss alles.   [lxxx].

This is a fine example of the indirect method of dramatic representation, more effective than the shrill cry of the demented but
clairvoyant Johann in the final scene of the play:

Bringt Wein her! Lustig! Wein! Das ist ein Spass zum
Totlachen! Wein! Der Teufel hatt' im Schlaf den beiden
Mit Kohlen die Gesichter angeschmiert.
Nun kennen sie sich wieder. Schurken! Wein!
Wir wollen eins drauf trinken! [lxxxi].

There is no objective proof in *Die Familie Schroffenstein* of the
actual existence of the evil spirit to which both Sylvester and Johann
refer. It is impossible for us to decide whether the moral weakness of
the characters is the only cause of the tragedy or whether they are at
least partly the victims of a demonic power outside. Kleist has left his
real intentions obscure probably because he had not achieved intellectual clarity on the important issues of life when he began to write his
play. He certainly did not wish to write a 'Schicksalstragödie' in the
ordinary sense of the term. But since his reading of Kant his mind was
obsessed by the realization of human weakness for which humanity
cannot be held altogether responsible and his drama therefore arouses
a sense of the misfortune rather than the moral guilt of his principal
characters. Fate overwhelms them with disaster, but it is not the fate
that we meet in Greek tragedy or in the dramas of Müllner and of
Zacharias Werner. The fate of the characters in *Die Familie Schroffenstein* is their inability, whether they have good intentions or not,
to perceive the truth of the situation in which they find themselves;
it is the inherent fallibility of mankind that is the ultimate cause of
their tragedy. They are the sole agents in the drama, since no visible
external power determines their actions. Yet, the lovers excepted,
they are never truly themselves when they act in response to their own

inner urge of hatred and distrust. They are blinded by passion and blindly pursue their perverted aims. When they have achieved their purpose they feel no satisfaction, but awake as after a dream in a dull stupor, lacking comprehension.

Such is Rupert's sense of frustration after killing Ottokar in mistake for Agnes:

> *Santing* Die Schlange hat ein zähes Leben. Doch
> Beschwör' ich's fast. Das Schwert steckt ihr im Busen.
> *Rupert* (fährt sich mit der Hand übers Gesicht)
> Warum denn tat ich's Santing? Kann ich es
> Doch gar nicht finden im Gedächtnis. —
> *Santing*   Ei,
> Es ist ja Agnes.
> *Rupert*   Agnes, ja, ganz recht,
> Die tat mir Böses, mir viel Böses, o,
> Ich weiss es wohl —Was war es schon?
> *Santing*   Ich weiss
> Nicht, wie du's meinst. Das Mädchen selber hat
> Nichts Böses dir getan.
> *Rupert*   Nichts Böses? Santing!
> Warum denn hätt' ich sie gemordet? Sage
> Mir schnell, ich bitte dich, womit sie mich
> Beleidigt, sag's recht hämisch — Basiliske,
> Sieh mich nicht an, sprich, Teufel, sprich, und weisst
> Du nichts, so lüg' es! [lxxxii].

This passage reveals the fortuity of Rupert's behaviour despite his single-mindedness. Impervious to the wiser counsel of his wife Eustache, but easily persuaded by his retainer Santing, he follows the path of hatred and of suspicion to its bewildering end. Obdurately seeking revenge and finally achieving it, he has to be reminded by Santing why he sought it. He is the victim of passion and the dupe of a mistaken sense of justice. Essentially he is more weak-willed than evil-minded. When Jeronimus has been killed at his behest, he feels remorse, but he blames not himself as much as Santing for obeying his command too readily:

> Das eben ist der Fluch der Macht, dass sich
> Dem Willen, dem leicht widerruflichen,
> Ein Arm gleich beut, der fest unwiderruflich
> Die Tat ankettet. Nicht ein Zehntteil würd'
> Ein Herr des Bösen tun, müsst' er es selbst
> Mit eignen Händen tun. Es heckt sein blosser

Gedanke Unheil aus, und seiner Knechte
Geringster hat den Vorteil über ihn,
Dass er das Böse wollen darf. [lxxxiii].

He refuses to take the responsibility for his own decisions and in
deference to Eustace imposes a sentence of imprisonment upon
Santing, but at the same time rewards him for his services:

> Es ist
> Mir widerlich, ich will's getan nicht haben.
> Auf deine Kappe nimm's — ich steck' dich in
> Den Schlossturm. —
>
> . . . . . .
>
> Kommst du heraus, das schöne
> Gebirgslehn wird dir nicht entgehn. [lxxxiv].

In the structure of the play the relations between Rupert and Santing
are a disconcerting element. They remind us of those between the
Prince and Marinelli in Lessing's *Emilia Galotti*, but whereas the depen-
dence of the ruler upon the fealty of his retainer is an essential part
of the tragic economy in the latter drama, in *Die Familie Schroffenstein*
it constitutes an ingredient that confounds the issue of the whole work.
It weakens the impression of inevitability which the tragedy is
designed to arouse, although Kleist may have intended to produce
the opposite result by means of this theme. He probably desired to
accentuate the quality of contingency in Rupert's guilt by making
him the victim of Santing's subserviency, but in doing this Kleist
adopted a principle of motivation which conflicts with that prevailing
in the rest of the play.

The basic fact of the tragedy in *Die Familie Schroffenstein* is the
inability of the characters to penetrate the mystery surrounding the
death of Peter. In their reaction to this circumstance and to the
circumstances arising from it, they reveal two attitudes of mind.
Either they believe the worst of the other members of the family
and suspect their motives from the beginning, or they rely on their
own benevolence, and distrust not those who are maligned but those
who malign them. The principal representatives of the former group
are Rupert and Sylvester's wife Gertrude, and of the latter group
Sylvester, Rupert's wife Eustache, and Agnes. Ottokar first belongs
to those who are misled by appearances and he takes the oath at
Rossitz to exterminate the members of the Warwand family. Later
he is converted by the sweet reasonableness of Agnes and he determines to solve the secret of Peter's death rather than act upon mere

suspicion. He is the only member of both families to follow up the one material clue that can explain what he now believes to be a ghastly mistake. When Agnes entreats him to pacify his father he recognizes the futility of such an undertaking and he resolves to seek a direct remedy of the feud by clearing up the mystery of Peter's death:

> Ich mildern? Meinen Vater? Gute Agnes,
> Er trägt uns, wie die See das Schiff, wir müssen
> Mit seiner Woge fort, sie ist nicht zu
> Beschwören. — Nein, ich wüsste wohl was Bessers.
> — Denn fruchtlos ist doch alles, kommt der Irrtum
> Ans Licht nicht, der uns neckt. —
>
> . . . . . .
> Nur einen Augenblick noch. — So wie einer,
> Kann auch der andre Irrtum schwinden. — Weisst
> Du was ich tun jetzt werde? Immer ist's
> Mir aufgefallen, dass an beiden Händen
> Der Bruderleiche just derselbe Finger,
> Der kleine Finger fehlte. — Mördern, denk'
> Ich, müsste jedes andre Glied fast wicht'ger
> Doch sein, als just der kleine Finger. Lässt
> Sich was erforschen, ist's nur an dem Ort
> Der Tat. Den weiss ich. Leute wohnen dort,
> Das weiss ich auch. — Ja recht, ich gehe hin. [lxxxv].

His effort comes near to success, but it is frustrated by the vengefulness of Rupert and Sylvester. Ottokar is the only character who adopts a rational method of inquiry. The others, even when they desire reconciliation rather than revenge, either remain inactive or become influential participants of the tragic developments. These noble characters derive their strength from one source, from the feeling of goodness and benevolence towards others, which they uphold, whatever obstacles they meet. Eustache affirms this fundamental faith when she says:

> Nun, über jedwedes Geständnis geht
> Mein innerstes Gefühl doch. [lxxxvi].

and Agnes shares her convictions:

> Denn etwas gibt's, das über alles Wähnen
> Und Wissen hoch erhaben — das Gefühl
> Ist es der Seelengüte andrer. [lxxxvii].

However ineffectual this feeling proves to be, it is the source of all that is best in human nature. The difference between Sylvester and Eustache on the one hand and Rupert and Gertrude on the other is the fact that the former possess this supreme human quality, whereas the latter are creatures of passion. Passion blinds and misleads human beings, feeling divines the truth even if it cannot unravel circumstances that hide the truth. The fundamental conflict between the characters in *Die Familie Schroffenstein* is not, as it has been stated, the conflict of Reason against Feeling so much as the opposition of Passion and Feeling. Rupert's and Gertrude's fault is not that they are too rational, but that they are too passionate, that they do not use their reason at all. Nor do Eustache and Sylvester exert their rational powers and hence they do not help to unravel the truth, Ottokar being the only man of common sense in the drama. Kleist knows at this early stage that feeling is a guide to truth, a knowledge that will prove effective at a later date as a basis for his newly-found optimism. Now the propinquity of his 'Kantian experience' obscured for him every possibility of successful human enterprise in the field of mutual understanding.

This tragic situation is shown most clearly in the case of Sylvester. In a drama that does not possess a protagonist or a single hero in the accepted sense of these terms, he is yet a character apart, more finely drawn than the others, and designed to arouse our sympathy in the greatest measure. He perceives the root cause of disorder in the human world more clearly than others. He rebukes his wife Gertrude for poisoning the mind of Agnes with tales of the wickedness of the house of Rossitz:

> Was ist das? Ich erstaun' — O, daran ist
> Beim Himmel! niemand schuld als du, Gertrude!
> Das Misstraun ist die schwarze Sucht der Seele,
> Und alles, auch das Schuldlos-Reine, zieht
> Fürs kranke Aug' die Tracht der Hölle an.
> Das Nichtsbedeutende, Gemeine, ganz
> Alltägliche, spitzfündig, wie zerstreute
> Zwirnfäden, wird's zu einem Bild geknüpft,
> Das uns mit grässlichen Gestalten schreckt. [lxxxviii].

He is the most tragic figure of the play because he loses his faith in humanity. His sweet trustfulness is turned into suspicion when he hears of Jeronimus' death in Rossitz. He tries to maintain his belief in Rupert's innocence and in his own ability to pacify him, but is compelled to renounce his faith. He becomes enmeshed in the vendetta of hatred and distrust and he slays his daughter just as Rupert kills his own son. With a fine touch of discrimination Kleist shows the overwhelming force of his grief at the end of the play. It is left to Rupert to appeal for reconciliation, while Sylvester in silent pain replies but with a gesture.

Kleist has endowed him with more sensibility than the other characters and in one respect has made him a model of dignity. Sylvester's swoon is a symptom not merely of physical weakness but also of spiritual strength. He can withdraw from the world and achieve closer contact with the ultimate springs of human life than other, more self-possessed human beings. After his swoon he refuses a restorative from his wife but trusts in his own spiritual vigour:

> *Sylvester*   Dein Bemühn
> Beschämt mich. Gönne mir zwei Augenblicke,
> So mach' ich alles wieder gut, und stelle
> Von selbst mich her.
> *Gertrude*   Zum mind'sten nimm die Tropfen
> Aus dem Tyrolerfläschchen, das du selbst
> Stets als ein heilsam Mittel mir gepriesen.
> *Sylvester* An eigne Kraft glaubt doch kein Weib, und traut
> Stets einer Salbe mehr zu als der Seele.
> *Gertrude* Es wird dich stärken, glaube mir. —
> *Sylvester*   Dazu
> Braucht's nichts als mein Bewusstsein. (Er steht auf)
>   Was mich freut
> Ist, dass der Geist doch mehr ist, als ich glaubte.
> Denn flieht er gleich auf einen Augenblick,
> An seinen Urquell geht er nur, zu Gott,
> Und mit Heroenkraft kehrt er zurück . . . [lxxxix].

These words, however, also show, as does the spirit of the whole drama, that the values which Kleist was to explain at a later date in his essay *Über das Marionettentheater* do not supply us with a key to the interpretation of *Die Familie Schroffenstein*. Whereas Sylvester emphasizes the beneficial power of consciousness ('Bewusstsein'), the perverting influence of this faculty is stressed in the essay. Kleist does not yet envisage that return of man to the state of innocence which he will be able to affirm later. In this connection the conversation between the blind Sylvius and the demented Johann in the last scene of *Die Familie Schroffenstein* possesses symbolical importance and it illuminates the deeper meaning of the drama:

Sylvius   Wohin führst du mich, Knabe?
Johann   Ins Elend, Alter, denn ich bin die Torheit.
Sei nur getrost! Es ist der rechte Weg.
Sylvius Weh! Weh! Im Wald die Blindheit, und ihr Hüter
Der Wahnsinn! Führe heim mich, Knabe, heim!
Johann Ins Glück? Es geht nicht, Alter. 's ist inwendig
Verriegelt. Komm. Wir müssen vorwärts.
Sylvius   Müssen wir?
So mögen sich die Himmlischen erbarmen.
Wohlan. Ich folge dir. [xc].

This pessimistic conception of the condition of man was expressed
even more clearly in *Die Familie Ghonorez* in the words of Rodrigo:

                                    O ihr Brüder
Verstossene des Schicksals, Hand in Hand
Hinaus ins Elend aus dem Paradiese,
Aus dem des Cherubs Flammenschwert uns treibt! [xci].

   The characters of Kleist's tragedy are not marionettes in the
idealized sense which he gives to this term in *Über das Marionettentheater*. They are guided by a Satanic power rather than a divine
force. Sylvester, of all the persons in the drama most eminently
endowed with fine perceptions, is puzzled by God's intentions,
although, as we have seen, he knows that God is the ultimate source of
man's strength. He cannot understand the ways of God, because God
allows so much confusion and error to reign in the world. Some
of his most characteristic utterances testify to this perplexity:

Jeronimus Aus diesem Wirrwarr finde sich ein Pfaffe!
Ich kann es nicht.
Sylvester   Ich bin dir wohl ein Rätsel?
Nicht wahr? Nun, tröste dich; Gott ist es mir. [xcii].

                              Gott der Gerechtigkeit!
Sprich deutlich mit dem Menschen, dass er's weiss
Auch, was er soll!   [xciii].

   When the tragic events of *Die Familie Schroffenstein* are viewed in
the light of this feeling of uncertainty, the drama reveals itself as a
true product of Kleist's pessimism. Unlike *Robert Guiskard* it is
ultimately the issue not of his literary but of his philosophical
experiences. To the detriment of the main design he did not entirely
overcome the temptation of imitating the work of other playwrights,
but intrinsically *Die Familie Schroffenstein* bears the authentic stamp of
originality. Unlike *Romeo and Juliet* it is a tragedy of hatred engen-

dered by error. Just as the underlying sense of fate differs in these two tragedies, so does the function of the love theme indicate a divergence of artistic purposes. It is the overriding interest in *Romeo and Juliet* and only a subordinate element in *Die Familie Schroffenstein*. The families are more important in Kleist, the lovers in Shakespeare. It has been well said that love is an obstacle to the prevailing hatred in *Die Familie Schroffenstein*, whereas in *Romeo and Juliet* the lovers are thwarted by the family feud. Kleist's is the fiercer theme. The reconciliation of his families at the end of the play must be seen against the gloomy background of guilt and confusion quite absent in Shakespeare's tragedy. Shakespeare dismisses us with a feeling of regret and with that aesthetic elation which only a true poet can excite. Kleist, lacking the power of imparting this highest artistic consolation, indelibly imprints horror and perplexity upon our minds. In the final scene it is only the blind Sylvius and the demented Johann who are able to recognize the truth, and after Ursula's apocalyptic appearance the whole tragedy stands revealed as a ghastly mistake, a grim spectacle of the infirmity and the factiousness of the human mind.

II

AMPHITRYON

IN *Die Familie Schroffenstein* man's tragic fallibility is revealed most strikingly when his soul is ruled by passion. Feeling, on the other hand, appears to offer an escape from error, although it is not a guarantee of salvation. In *Amphitryon*, Kleist's next drama, feeling even of the purest kind is shown to be fallible, and whereas in *Die Familie Schroffenstein* the fault seems to lie partly with the human beings for failing to exercise their reason, in the latter work Amphitryon and Alkmene make every rational effort to unravel the secret confronting them, without success. However, the circumstances which produce this confusion of mind are of the most exceptional order; the god who intervenes in the lives of the Theban warrior and his wife creates so singular a situation, that only with the greatest caution can we draw general conclusions from the experiences of Kleist's characters and consider to what extent he thought them typical of the destiny of all human beings.

His choice of this particular comedy by Molière and his alteration of its dramatic content clearly show that his mind was still filled with his earlier apprehensions. By making additions to the plot and by shifting the emphasis of the Greek story, he produced what is in effect a tragedy rather than a comedy, although he described it as 'a comedy after Molière'.

Little is known of the genesis of Kleist's play, which appeared in 1807. There is no evidence to support the view that it originated during Kleist's stay in Paris. He probably began his work not earlier than 1806, when he was occupied with adapting the writings of other French authors, e.g. La Fontaine. In 1804 J. D. Falk published a version of Plautus' *Amphitruo*, one year after a new translation of this work had appeared in Germany. It is unlikely that Kleist was influenced by either of these publications, although his play has one feature in common with Falk's comedy, Alkmene's choice of Jupiter when she is faced with the two Amphitryons in Act V. Nor is it probable that Kleist derived any assistance from his friend Zschokke, whose translations of Molière (*Molières Lustspiele und Possen in deutscher Bearbeitung*) appeared during 1805 and 1806, but who did not include the *Amphitryon* in his collection.

Probably none of the many versions of the legend that are to be found in Spanish, French, English and German literature from the sixteenth to the eighteenth century, except that by Molière, was known to Kleist. It is certainly most unlikely that he had heard of a remarkable work published in Lüneburg in 1621, Burmeister's *Plauti Renati sive Sacri Mater Virgo*,[1] in which the author presents a Christianized version of the Greek legend, 'Comoedia prima ex Amphitruone ad Admirandum Conceptionis et Incarnationis Filii Dei Misterium inversa'. It is a very rare book and this should be borne in mind when one assesses the validity of the opinion which was first advanced by Adam Müller and which has since then been adopted by several critics. Writing about Kleist's drama in a letter to Gentz, he says: 'Der Amphitryon handelt ja wohl ebensogut von der unbefleckten Empfängnis der heiligen Jungfrau, als von dem Geheimnis der Liebe überhaupt, und so ist er gerade aus der hohen, schönen Zeit entsprungen, in der sich endlich die Einheit alles Glaubens, aller Liebe und die grosse, innere Gemeinschaft aller Religionen aufgetan.' [xciv].[2] This view is echoed by Goethe who, according to a report by Riemer, believed that Kleist's drama 'enthält nichts Geringeres, als eine Deutung der Fabel ins Christliche, in die Überschattung der Maria vom Heiligen Geist.' [xcv].[3]

This interpretation is more ingenious than correct. If it is pushed to its logical conclusion, the absurdness of the conjecture becomes at once apparent. The story of Kleist's drama is, after all, a tale of seduction and even the promise which Jupiter makes to Amphitryon at the end of the play:

> Dir wird ein Sohn geboren werden,
> Dess' Name Herkules [xcvi]

cannot seriously be considered the parallel of the holy Annunciation. Jupiter pacifies Amphitryon rather than Alkmene, and he does so only after Amphitryon, quoting precedent, requests the favour as his due for services rendered:

> Nein, Vater Zeus, zufrieden bin ich nicht!
> Und meines Herzens Wunsche wächst die Zunge.
> Was du dem Tyndarus getan, tust du
> Auch dem Amphitryon: Schenk' einen Sohn
> Gross, wie die Tyndariden, ihm. [xcvii].

[1] Cf. K. v. Reinhardstoettner: *Plautus. Spätere Bearbeitungen plautinischer Lustspiele*, 1886, p. 208 *passim*.

[2] May 25, 1807. It has been pointed out that Adam Müller, though a convert to Catholicism, confused the immaculate conception of Mary with the virgin birth of Christ.

[3] Biedermann: *Goethes Gespräche*, Vol. I, p. 503.

Goethe justifiably considered this final development 'klatrig', in bad taste, and he clearly perceived the underlying tragedy which invalidates his own view of the Christian parallel: 'Der wahre Amphitryon muss es sich gefallen lassen, dass ihm Zeus diese Ehre angetan hat. Sonst ist die Situation der Alkmene peinlich und die des Amphitryon zuletzt grausam.' [xcviii].[1] Indeed, Goethe fully appreciated the essentially tragic nature of Kleist's work and the peculiar quality of its dramatic problem: 'Der antike Sinn in Behandlung des Amphitryons ging auf Verwirrung der Sinne, auf den Zwiespalt der Sinne mit der Überzeugung ... Der gegenwärtige, Kleist, geht bei den Hauptpersonen auf die Verwirrung des Gefühls hinaus'. [xcix].[2] This is a precise description of the drama, except that 'Verwirrung der Sinne' forms an important part of its content too. Kleist was certainly more interested in the emotional reactions of his characters to the deception played upon them than in the deception itself, but he did not neglect this aspect. He even enhanced it by making an alteration in the material which Molière had presented. The substitution of the initial J for the original A on the diadem that Amphitryon sends to Alkmene is an invention of Kleist. He made this addition in order to intensify the confusion in the minds of both characters, particularly in Alkmene.

Whereas in the French comedy Amphitryon is the more important character, in the German play Alkmene occupies the centre of the dramatic interest. In Molière's work the relations between Jupiter and Alcmène are far less significant than those between him and the Theban general. She disappears from the scene when the climax is reached and she therefore takes no part in the dénouement of the drama. The rôle which she plays in Kleist's work on the other hand necessitates her reappearance at the most vital point of the action— at the moment when Jupiter reveals his identity. The full weight of tragic responsibility rests upon her when she is compelled to choose between the false and the real Amphitryon and her suffering is more intense than that of her bewildered husband, when the true facts of the situation are made known.

Kleist also changed an earlier portion of Molière's comedy with a similar end in view. Unlike the heroine in the French play Alkmene remains ignorant of Jupiter's true identity until the end of the drama and the fourth and fifth scenes of the second Act are designed to reveal the tragic aspect of her character. These scenes bear little relation to the equivalent portions of the original. They are virtually Kleist's own invention and they show where his real interest in the

---

[1] Biedermann: *Goethes Gespräche*, Vol. I, p. 503.   [2] Goethe's Diary, July 13, 1807.

Amphitryon legend lay. The fourth scene demonstrates Alkmene's 'Verwirrung der Sinne', the fifth her 'Verwirrung des Gefühls'.

So great is the purity of her love for Amphitryon that she does not distinguish between the feelings aroused in her by him and those which Jupiter had excited on the previous night. Her very innocence is her weakness. She is not assailed by doubt until Amphitryon expresses his own misgivings. Then she recollects the harsh words which Jupiter had used to describe her husband. He had endeavoured in vain to seduce her mind by discriminating between the lover and the husband, whom he calls 'a poltroon' and 'the vainglorious Theban general'. After her encounter with Amphitryon in Act II she is reminded of these taunts and she loses her sense of assurance. This confusion borders on bewilderment when she realizes that the diadem contains the letter J:

> Wie soll ich Worte finden, meine Charis,
> Das Unerklärliche dir zu erklären?
> Da ich bestürzt mein Zimmer wieder finde,
> Nicht wissend, ob ich wache, ob ich träume,
> Wenn sich die rasende Behauptung wagt,
> Dass mir ein anderer erschienen sei;
>
> . . . .
>
> Da ich jetzt frage: hast du wohl geirrt?
> Denn einen äfft der Irrtum doch von beiden,
> Nicht ich, nicht er, sind einer Tücke fähig;
> Und jener doppelsinn'ge Scherz mir jetzt
> Durch das Gedächtnis zuckt, da der Geliebte,
> Amphitryon, ich weiss nicht, ob du's hörtest,
> Mir auf Amphitryon den Gatten schmähte,
> Wie Schaudern jetzt, Entsetzen mich ergreift
> Und alle Sinne treulos von mir weichen, —
> Fass' ich, o du Geliebte, diesen Stein,
> Das einzig unschätzbare, teure Pfand,
> Das ganz untrüglich mir zum Zeugnis dient.   [c].

She is horrified and terror-stricken, her senses have begun to betray her, but she is still conscious of her emotional integrity and she affirms her faith in the infallibility of her love:

> Ist diese Hand mein? Diese Brust hier mein?
> Gehört das Bild mir, das der Spiegel strahlt?
> Er wäre fremder mir, als ich! Nimm mir
> Das Aug', so hör' ich ihn; das Ohr, ich fühl' ihn;
> Mir das Gefühl hinweg, ich atm' ihn noch;

Nimm Aug' und Ohr, Gefühl mir und Geruch,
Mir alle Sinn' und gönne mir das Herz:
So lässt du mir die Glocke, die ich brauche,
Aus einer Welt noch find' ich ihn heraus. [ci].

The tragedy of Alkmene is more clearly revealed when we compare her predicament with that of Littegarde in Kleist's short story
Der Zweikampf. After Friedrich had been defeated in the duel which
he fought to prove Littegarde's innocence, he exhorts her to remain
steadfast although the judgment of God had gone against her: 'O meine
teuerste Littegarde', rief der Kämmerer: 'bewahre deine Sinne vor
Verzweiflung! türme das Gefühl, das in deiner Brust lebt, wie einen
Felsen empor: halte dich daran und wanke nicht, und wenn Erd'
und Himmel unter dir und über dir zu Grunde gingen! Lass uns,
von zwei Gedanken, die die Sinne verwirren, den verständlicheren
und begreiflicheren denken, und ehe du dich schuldig glaubst, lieber
glauben, dass ich in dem Zweikampf, den ich für dich gefochten,
siegte! — Gott, Herr meines Lebens' setzte er in diesem Augenblick
hinzu, indem er seine ·Hände vor sein Antlitz legte, 'bewahre meine
Seele selbst vor Verwirrung!' [cii].

Littegarde's and Friedrich's minds are perplexed, but their feeling
remains unimpaired. Alkmene has to face a graver ordeal, when her
senses begin to betray her. The time will come when her trust in her
heart will be shattered just as her confidence in external reality has
been shaken. For the moment, however, she only perceives the
incompatibility of outward appearances with her inward conviction:

Nicht nur entblösst bin ich von jedem Zeugnis,
Ein Zeugnis wider mich ist dieser Stein.
Was kann ich, ich Verwirrte, dem entgegnen?

. . . . . .

Bin ich wohl sicher, sprich, dass ich auch gestern
Das Zeichen, das hier steht, von ihm empfing? [ciii].

The following scene of Act II, in which Alkmene's relations with
Jupiter reach their climax, shows that she is again not able to distinguish between him and Amphitryon, although her suspicions have
been aroused, and that in spite of Jupiter's attempts to explain the
situation to her, her devotion to Amphitryon betrays her once more.
Zeus praises her 'infallible feeling' and the 'golden scales' of her
sensibility, but it is this faculty that fails her. She is aware of the
heightened feeling which the god inspires in her. She had admitted to
this intenser joy in the fourth scene of Act II:

> Ich hätte für sein Bild ihn halten können,
> Für sein Gemälde, sieh, von Künstlershand,
> Dem Leben treu, ins Göttliche verzeichnet.
> Er stand, ich weiss nicht, vor mir, wie im Traum,
> Und ein unsägliches Gefühl ergriff
> Mich meines Glücks, wie ich es nie empfunden . . . [civ].

The only difference which she senses between the emotion aroused in her by Amphitryon and that by Jupiter is one of degree. Yet it is just this awareness of a difference that finally leads to her tragic rejection of the real Amphitryon. Jupiter, having failed to seduce her by suggesting a distinction between lover and husband, now plays on her exalted love. Once more he does not succeed in his purpose. Neither by intimating the true state of affairs, nor by cajolery or threats does he really win Alkmene's love. He reveals his knowledge of her profoundest secret that even when she prays to Zeus the image of Amphitryon is always before her:

> Wer ist's, dem du an seinem Altar betest?
> Ist er's dir wohl, der über Wolken ist?
> Kann dein befanger Sinn ihn wohl erfassen?
> Kann dein Gefühl, an seinem Nest gewöhnt,
> Zu solchem Fluge wohl die Schwingen wagen?
> Ist's nicht Amphitryon, der Geliebte, stets,
> Vor welchem du im Staube liegst? [cv].

He elicits from her a promise that she will in future think of Zeus alone in her devotions:

> Gut, gut, du sollst mit mir zufrieden sein.
> Es soll in jeder ersten Morgenstunde
> Auch kein Gedanke fürder an dich denken . . . [cvi].

but she rejects his suggestion that she might abandon Amphitryon for him. Jupiter realizes that he has been defeated by Alkmene's single-mindedness and exclaims

> Verflucht der Wahn, der mich hieher gelockt! [cvii].

Alkmene has resisted the temptation which Zeus offered her. And yet in one respect he does succeed. Her integrity is untouched, but the balance of her emotions becomes disturbed. Her feelings are entangled and she is enticed into making a confession that amounts to an involuntary betrayal of Amphitryon. By reiterating the divine claims upon her affection, Zeus implants doubts and confusion in her mind:

> Ach, ich Unsel'ge, wie verwirrst du mich.
> Kann man auch Unwillkürliches verschulden? [cviii].

Then, by depicting the pathetic and extravagant yearnings of the lonely god thirsting for the love of mortal woman and by suggesting with egregious flattery that she might be chosen by fate to return the thanks which all the created millions owe their creator, Jupiter induces her to surrender:

> Ward ich so heil'gem **Amte** auserkoren,
> Er, der mich schuf, er walte über mich! [cix].

Yet even this acquiescence is not the declaration of love he had sought and so he resorts ignobly to pretence and prevarication. Exploiting the exaltation which she feels in his presence, he extracts an admission that betokens a rift in her affections for Amphitryon and the loss of her emotional equipoise. This scene represents the veritable seduction of Alkmene, and, at the same time, Jupiter's most signal defeat:

> *Jupiter* Wenn ich nun dieser Gott dir wär' — ?
> *Alkmene*   Wenn du
> — Wie ist mir denn? Wenn du mir dieser Gott wärst
> — Ich weiss nicht, soll ich vor dir niederfallen,
> Soll ich es nicht? Bist du's mir? Bist du's mir?
> *Jupiter* Entscheide du. Amphitryon bin ich.
> *Alkmene* Amphitryon —
> *Jupiter*   Amphitryon, dir ja.
> Doch wenn ich, frag' ich, dieser Gott dir wäre,
> Dir liebend vom Olymp herabgestiegen,
> Wie würdest du dich dann zu fassen wissen?
> *Alkmene* Wenn du mir, Liebster, dieser Gott wärst — ja,
> So wüsst' ich nicht, wo mir Amphitryon wäre,
> So würd' ich folgen dir, wohin du gehst,
> Und wär's auch, wie Euridike, zum Orkus.
> *Jupiter* Wenn du nicht wüsstest, wo Amphitryon wäre.
> Doch wie, wenn sich Amphitryon jetzt zeigte?
> *Alkmene* Wenn sich Amphitryon mir — ach, du quälst mich.
> Wie kann sich auch Amphitryon mir zeigen,
> Da ich Amphitryon in Armen halte?
> *Jupiter* Und dennoch könnt'st du leicht den Gott in Armen halten,
> Im Wahn, es sei Amphitryon.
> Warum soll dein Gefühl dich überraschen?
> Wenn ich, der Gott, dich hier umschlungen hielte,
> Und jetzo dein Amphitryon sich zeigte,
> Wie würd' dein Herz sich wohl erklären?
> *Alkmene* Wenn du, der Gott, mich hier umschlungen hieltest,

E

> Und jetzo sich Amphitryon mir zeigte,
> Ja — dann so traurig würd' ich sein, und wünschen,
> Dass er der Gott mir wäre, und dass du
> Amphitryon mir bliebst, wie du es bist. [cx].

Although Jupiter cannot win Alkmene except by pretending that he is Amphitryon, he has at last succeeded in compelling her to admit the superiority of the lover over the husband. The situation is intensely ironical, in the tragic rather than the comic sense of the term. Kleist interpolated this scene at the critical juncture of the dramatic action and thus by shifting the emphasis from Amphitryon to Alkmene changed what was originally a comic predicament into a tragic dilemma.

Nearly until the end of the play Amphitryon, too, is a tragic figure, but his suffering is different from that of Alkmene and the explanation of the true situation as well as Jupiter's promise that Alkmene will give birth to a son destined for eternal fame, bring him entire relief. Alkmene's trials, on the other hand, mount to the very end of the drama. The final developments are not a welcome solution for her as they are for Amphitryon, but a truly tragic catastrophe. He suffers because his honour is at stake and because his mind is afflicted by unutterable confusion: 'Kann man's begreifen' he exclaims ''reimen? Kann man's fassen?' [cxi].

> Ich habe sonst von Wundern schon gehört,
> Von unnatürlichen Erscheinungen, die sich
> Aus einer andern Welt hieher verlieren;
> Doch heute knüpft der Faden sich von jenseits
> An meine Ehre und erdrosselt sie. [cxii].

> Dass ein Betrug vorhanden ist, ist klar,
> Wenn meine Sinn' auch das fluchwürdige
> Gewebe noch nicht fassen. [cxiii].

His ordeal reaches its climax when the very identity of his personality is denied, when he is in danger of losing even the sense of the oneness of his being. He never doubts Alkmene's integrity and innocence and her verdict sets the seal upon his self-annihilation:

> Wenn sie als Gatten ihn erkennen kann,
> So frag' ich nichts danach mehr, wer ich bin:
> So will ich ihn Amphitryon begrüssen. [cxiv].

> Jetzt einen Eid selbst auf den Altar schwör' ich,
> Und sterbe siebenfachen Todes gleich,
> Des unerschütterlich erfassten Glaubens,
> Dass er Amphitryon ihr ist. [cxv].

When Jupiter, however, reassures him, his restoration is permanent and complete. To Alkmene the final revelation brings no relief. Her feelings have become so entangled by the sophistry and the allurements of Jupiter that with fearful words she spurns the real Amphitryon when she is confronted with him in the presence of his divinely impersonated form:

> Du Ungeheu'r! Mir scheusslicher,
> Als es geschwollen in Morästen nistet! [cxvi].

She realizes now that she had given herself to another Amphitryon and she believes that this other being was a visitation from Hell that beguiled her senses and confounded her love:

> Jetzt erst, was für ein Wahn mich täuscht', erblick' ich.
> Der Sonne heller Lichtglanz war mir nötig,
> Solch einen feilen Bau gemeiner Knechte
> Vom Prachtwuchs dieser königlichen Glieder,
> Den Farren von dem Hirsch zu unterscheiden!
> Verflucht die Sinne, die so gröblichem
> Betrug erliegen! O verflucht der Busen,
> Der solche falschen Töne gibt!
> Verflucht die Seele, die nicht soviel taugt,
> Um ihren eigenen Geliebten sich zu merken! [cxvii].

She truly believes that she is choosing the real Amphitryon and is rejecting his satanic counterfeit, whereas in fact she spurns her husband in favour of his hypostatic self. Once again she is the victim of a supremely ironical and tragic illusion. On the former occasions her guilt had been negative. When Jupiter had appeared to her she had not recognized him as another being. Now she errs positively. She chooses the false and reviles the true Amphitryon. The curse which she pronounces on her senses, her feelings and her soul is more appropriate to her present than to her past failure. In these circumstances her monosyllabic exclamation 'Ach' when the Theban generals express their jubilation, cannot denote a joyful anticipation of the promised birth of Hercules. Nor is it an articulation of relief, 'ein Seufzer der Erleichterung'.[1] It is, rather, a compressed utterance of overwhelming despair and confusion.

The view that Kleist's *Amphitryon* ends on a note of complete reconciliation becomes tenable only if one accepts a literal interpretation of his own description 'ein Lustspiel nach Molière'. His alterations comprise only about one-third of Molière's work. He has

[1] H. Meyer-Benfey: *Das Drama Heinrich von Kleists.*

added no new characters, and has retained the burlesque sub-plot. While Jupiter assumes the shape of Amphitryon, Mercury appears in the form of his servant Sosias and taunts him mercilessly. This farcical action had an appropriate place in the work when it was the concomitant of a purely comic action. It had its proper function in the French drama, where such a parallel episode underlines the idea of the play. The burlesque in Kleist's play is too noisy and violent an accompaniment of the serious action to serve a similar aesthetic purpose. As characters Sosias and Charis are indispensable; they are an integral part of the *mise en scène*. But their rôles have expanded beyond the requirements of the drama. Unlike the comic characters of Shakespeare's tragedies they endanger the design of the work as a whole. Goethe disliked the mixture of styles in Kleist's drama. He felt that they were not fused into a consistent unity.

It cannot be said, however, that the particular quality of the comedy presented in *Amphitryon* was merely the result of Kleist's imitation of Molière. It is found again in *Der Zerbrochene Krug*, a work which has few traces of its author's indebtedness to German writers.[1] Furthermore, although the plot of this comedy contains elements of tragedy, they are strictly subordinated to the main design. This play, therefore, reveals a marked advance in Kleist's dramatic technique.

[1] J. H. Krumpelmann has shown the remarkable affinities between Kleist's comedy and Shakespeare's *Measure for Measure*, as well as with the Falstaffian dramas. Cf. bibliography.

III

DER ZERBROCHENE KRUG

IN a prefatory note to his short story *Der Zerbrochene Krug*, Heinrich Zschokke gives the following account of the origin of Kleist's comedy and of his own tale: 'Man kennt, unter gleichem Namen, ein kleines Stück vom Dichter des "Kätchen von Heilbronn." Dieses und die folgende Erzählung hatten im Jahre 1802 zu Bern einerlei Veranlassung des Entstehens. Heinrich von Kleist und Ludwig Wieland, des Dichters Sohn, pflogen Freundschaft mit dem Verfasser, in dessen Zimmer ein Kupferstich, "La cruche cassée," unterschrieben, hing . . . Die ausdrucksvolle Zeichnung belustigte und verlockte zu mancherlei Deutungen des Inhalts. Im Scherz gelobten die Drei, jeder wollte seine eigentümliche Ansicht schriftlich ausführen. Ludwig Wieland verhiess eine Satire; Heinrich von Kleist entwarf sein Lustspiel, und der Verfasser gegenwärtiger Erzählung das, was hier gegeben wird.'[1] [cxviii]. The scene of Zschokke's tale is the country-side of the Provence. It is the story of Mariette's love for Colin and of her mother's vain attempt to force her to marry the rascally local judge Hautmartin.

The picture to which Zschokke refers has been identified as an engraving by Jean Jacques Le Veau after an unknown painting by Louis Philibert Debucourt.[2] Kleist has given a description of the picture in a preface which he wrote for his comedy but which he omitted to publish. This report is instructive, since it sheds light on the features of the engraving which particularly attracted Kleist's attention. If we remember that he began to write the drama in 1802, at the time when he was still occupied with the composition of *Robert Guiskard*, but did not complete it until 1806, (it was performed at Weimar and some of the scenes printed in the *Phöbus* of 1808), the preface will help us to determine the place which this comedy occupies in the main body of his dramatic work.

'Diesem Lustspiel' Kleist wrote in his preface. 'liegt wahrscheinlich ein historisches Faktum, worüber ich jedoch keine nähere Auskunft habe auffinden können, zum Grunde. Ich nahm die Veranlassung dazu aus einem Kupferstich, den ich vor mehreren Jahren in der Schweiz

---

[1] *Ausgewählte Novellen und Dichtungen*, 4. Teil, 1836, p. 133.
[2] A reproduction of the picture may be found in F. Servaes: *Heinrich von Kleist*, 1902, p. 75.

sah. Man bemerkte darauf — zuerst einen Richter, der gravitätisch auf dem Richterstuhl sass: vor ihm stand eine alte Frau, die einen zerbrochenen Krug hielt, sie schien das Unrecht, das ihm widerfahren war, zu demonstrieren: Beklagter, ein junger Bauerkerl, den der Richter, als überwiesen, andonnerte, verteidigte sich noch, aber schwach: ein Mädchen, das wahrscheinlich in dieser Sache gezeugt hatte (denn wer weiss, bei welcher Gelegenheit das Deliktum geschehen war) spielte sich, in der Mitte zwischen Mutter und Bräutigam, an der Schürze; wer ein falsches Zeugnis abgelegt hätte, könnte nicht zerknirschter dastehn: und der Gerichtsschreiber sah (er hatte vielleicht kurz vorher das Mädchen angesehen) jetzt den Richter misstrauisch zur Seite an, wie Kreon, bei einer ähnlichen Gelegenheit, den Oedip, als die Frage war, wer den Lajus erschlagen? Darunter stand: der zerbrochene Krug. — Das Original war, wenn ich nicht irre, von einem niederländischen Meister.' [cxix].

In Le Veau's engraving the judge does not appear as the guilty person. It is usually assumed that the boy and the girl are responsible for the breaking of the jug. Perhaps a secret meeting between them was the occasion of the accident. Presumably the judge is to find out what really occurred and the affair of the two lovers is thus revealed.

If this is the story which the picture tells, Kleist has completely altered it both in his description and in his play. The guilty person in the comedy is Richter Adam, who has tried to seduce Eve by promising to use his influence on behalf of her fiancé, Ruprecht. He is surprised by Ruprecht himself when he visits Eve in her room, and in the ensuing scuffle receives several bruises. In his flight he loses his wig and breaks a jug, but makes good his escape. On the following morning Eve's mother brings an action against Ruprecht whom she accuses of causing the damage. The play opens with the notary Licht's discovery of Adam's bruises and with his announcement of the impending visit of Gerichtsrat Walter, who has been sent on a circuit to inquire into the administration of justice in the Dutch provinces. The greater portion of the comedy consists of the trial conducted by Adam, in which he endeavours to cover up the truth about the previous night's happenings by casting suspicion on Ruprecht. Eve assists him, for she will not tell the true story of the incident. She still believes that Ruprecht has been posted to the East Indies and that the judge can prevent his being sent abroad. The exposure of Adam's guilt is brought about by the testimony of Brigitte, Walter's watchfulness, and Licht's interventions.

When we examine the function of these three characters, Brigitte,

Walter and Licht, the significance of Kleist's remark that the notary
in the engraving looks at the judge 'wie Kreon bei einer ähnlichen
Gelegenheit den Oedip', becomes clear. His comedy is, in effect, a
dramatization of the situation with which he had contended for so
long in writing *Robert Guiskard.* Just as Œdipus presides over the
gradual disclosure of the true state of affairs in which he appears as
the guilty person, so Adam conducts the trial which establishes his
own culpability. Likewise both in *Robert Guiskard* and in *Der Zerbrochene Krug* we observe the spectacle of an unsuccessful attempt on
the part of the principal figure to prevent the divulgence of a secret.
It may, therefore, be said that the notary Licht fulfils the function
which Abälard was to perform in the projected *Robert Guiskard.*
and which Kreon does perform in *Œdipus.* The characters invented
by Kleist (they are not represented in the picture, nor are they found
in Zschokke's story) serve a similar purpose. Gerichtsrat Walter
and Brigitte are embodiments of Fate in the world of mundane
events. By the judgment of the one and the testimony of the other,
Adam is convicted.

    Der Zerbrochene Krug, therefore, represents an interesting experiment
on the part of Kleist. He treated in the comic manner a theme that
he had originally conceived for a tragedy. This shows how closely
tragedy and comedy were related in his mind, an affinity not successfully demonstrated in *Amphitryon*, since in that play he merely
adapted the production of another dramatist for his own purposes.

    We must, however, ask ourselves by what criteria comedy can be
distinguished from tragedy in Kleist's work. If the two genres are
not distinguishable by their themes, the difference between them must
be sought in the treatment of these themes. Kleist's tragedies are
symbolical representations, they record individual instances of
universal human misfortune. A certain spaciousness is required in
the characters as well as the setting of a drama if it is to fulfil this
symbolic function, and he, therefore, except in *Die Familie Schroffenstein*, selected legendary, mythical and historical subjects for his
tragedies. In his comedy Kleist did not aim at achieving symbolical
representation. Bereft of this dignity it possesses merely idiosyncratic
significance. It does not treat the larger issues of life, but only a
particular example of human behaviour. Kleist wrongly believed that
the original of Le Veau's engraving was the work of a Dutch master.
In *Der Zerbrochene Krug* he presented a peasant scene in the manner
of the Dutch school of painting. He chose a trivial occasion and
petty characters and treated them with an attention to detail not to

be found in his tragedies. The sentiments, interests, desires, quarrels and the self-esteem of these characters are of the most limited kind and they are laughable because they are seriously expressed. The naturalistic portrayal of human life in its most restricted aspects is a feature that distinguishes Kleist's comedy from his tragedies.

Kleist's characters and their lives are comic because of their human insignificance rather than their social inferiority. In some of his prose tales, especially in *Michael Kohlhaas*, he portrayed the tragic fate of humble men and women. This shows that he did not consider social rank a criterion of the difference between tragedy and comedy. The effect produced by an action was a test that possessed greater validity for him. If an action had important consequences of a painful kind, it was suitable for representation in a tragedy. If a similar action did not transcend the sphere of common interest, it was more appropriately treated in the comic manner.[1]

There is another difference between *Robert Guiskard* and *Michael Kohlhaas* on the one hand, and *Der Zerbrochene Krug* on the other hand. The principal figures in these works are culpable, but each in a different way. To begin with, Kohlhaas is not guilty at all. He becomes guilty because he loses his sense of proportion and adopts violent measures to redress what is, in effect, a petty wrong. This wrong has been inflicted on him and he seeks to satisfy his undeniably legitimate sense of justice. To a large extent Guiskard is responsible for his guilt. His conduct is determined by his own ambition as much as by the occurrence of unforeseen events. But he is not guilty of committing a crime. Adam is reprehensible because he has committed an action of this kind. He has done wrong in pursuing a base desire rather than a noble project. He is deceitful in attempting to cover up his guilt and he tries to incriminate others in his endeavour to prevent the exposure of his own crime. In the circumscribed conditions of the play Adam's prevarications, his inventiveness and resourcefulness, his writhing and wriggling are comic because they are unsuccessful. It is for Kleist a laughable spectacle when a man deceitfully tries to hide his guilt but by his very efforts to escape detection reveals his culpability. The comedy of *Der Zerbrochene Krug* possesses this rather discomfiting quality. Satire, wit, repartee, verbal quibbles and play upon words all contribute to the humour of the work. The principal ingredient, however, is the ironical situation of a petty malefactor presiding over his own discomfiture.

[1] A similar instance may be found in the case of *Prinz Friedrich von Homburg*. On October 4, 1810, Kleist published in the *Berliner Abendblätter*, an anecdote entitled *Der Verlegne Magistrat* which amounts to a parody of the drama.

The ironical nature of Adam's position, the fact that he is compelled to function as the investigator of his own crime, imparts a property to the dramatic action which shows the correspondence between Kleist's comedy and his tragedies. This analogy exists despite the fundamental dissimilarity of the two genres in his work. If Gerichtsrat Walter had not been present at the trial, Adam might have succeeded in bullying Ruprecht and Eve into acquiescence. Kleist invented the figure of the commissioner of justice in order to introduce the element of compulsion into the dramatic action of his comedy, just as he used the device of external interference in *Amphitryon*.

A comparison of Jupiter in *Amphitryon* with Walter and Adam in *Der Zerbrochene Krug* will reveal the difference between Kleist's tragic and his comic treatment of, essentially, the same theme. Jupiter's rôle combines in itself aspects of the parts played by Walter and Adam. Like the former he intervenes in the lives of others, and like the latter he practises deceit. When he explains the motives of his intervention and his deceit (in the fifth scene of Act II) he nearly becomes a comic figure in Kleist's sense of the term. He is only saved from appearing ridiculous by his supreme position and by the fact that he voluntarily reveals his deceit. He is not subject to a higher power, since he intervenes in the lives of men like fate itself. For a comic treatment of the theme of deceit Kleist had to separate it from that of external interference and he had to embody the two themes in two different rôles.

Another difference between *Amphitryon* and *Der Zerbrochene Krug* is discovered when we compare Jupiter and Adam in their relations to Alkmene and Eve respectively. Adam fails where Jupiter succeeds because he is defeated by the petty circumstances of human life which a god is able to transcend. Jupiter cannot be surprised by the accident that ruins Adam's chances. Adam is successful in beguiling Eve's mind just as Jupiter misleads Alkmene, but he is prevented from exploiting his advantage. The fundamental difference between the two dramas is a difference of interest. The central theme of *Amphitryon* is Alkmene's tragic confusion resulting from Jupiter's impersonation, the subject-matter of *Der Zerbrochene Krug* is the unmasking of Adam's attempt to seduce Eve. Conscious deceit unsuccessfully employed is the topic of the comedy, unconscious error, a result of wilful deception, is the theme of the tragedy.

The tragic theme of error, however, is also touched upon in *Der Zerbrochene Krug*. The relationship of Eve and Ruprecht is compromised by Adam's knavery. Amphitryon's faith in Alkmene's innocence remains steadfast despite extreme provocation. Ruprecht, not knowing Eve's motives in refusing to disclose the identity of her visitor and having himself surprised her in the company of the man, suspects her of infidelity. His love is momentarily changed to hatred, but she wins back his love when the truth is established. If Adam's guilt had not been proven, Eve would have become a tragic figure. Her very attempt to keep Ruprecht near her would have resulted in her losing him. This issue is, however, not a serious one and it is entirely removed by the solution of the dramatic complications.[1]

This solution does not indicate a growth of optimism in Kleist. The fact that *Der Zerbrochene Krug* is a comedy does not mean that he had revised his attitude to life when he wrote the work. His pessimistic view of human nature subsisted, as is shown by his next drama, *Penthesilea*. The theme which had been touched upon in the comedy, the mutability of love under the influence of suspicion, becomes a dominant motif in this tragedy.

---

[1] In an earlier version of the final scenes, printed in *Phöbus*, Kleist had elaborated this aspect. He curtailed it considerably in the final version.

IV

PENTHESILEA

KLEIST occupies an unusual position in German literature at the beginning of the nineteenth century. Nearly every great poet or critic from Lessing to Hölderlin played his part in the development of German Hellenism which is an aspect of the Idealist movement in Germany. Kant's influence on Kleist showed that Kleist was not an adherent of this movement. Jean Paul was the only other important writer who did not subscribe to the tenets of Idealism and neither he nor Kleist contributed to the growth of Hellenism in Germany. Kleist may have understood the importance of Schlegel's discovery of the Dionysian element in Greek culture and used this new perception in his own work.[1] But *Penthesilea* is not an interpretation of a legend in the same sense as Goethe's *Iphigenie auf Tauris*. It does not offer an idealized picture of life or suggest a generally applicable solution of human conflicts.

Penthesilea has much in common with Iphigenie. The lives of both women are dominated, at a crucial juncture, by two supreme realities: subjective desire and the divine will. The fundamental difference between the two dramas, however, is revealed by the contrast in the valuation given to these elements in the plays. In Goethe's work the will of the gods and that of the heroine together effect the solution of nearly all the conflicts, while in Kleist's drama subjective desire and the divine will are in conflict and this conflict leads to the utter disintegration of the heroine's character.

Kleist began to write *Penthesilea* in 1806. A copy of the first draft of the work, dating from the end of the year 1807, has been preserved. In January 1808 Kleist published an excerpt entitled 'Organisches Fragment' in *Phöbus*. The complete work, revised and altered in many parts, appeared in 1808. These alterations are of considerable interest. In some respects they clarified the meaning of the drama, in other respects they obscured it by accentuating an aspect of the action hitherto not emphasized. Kleist's lack of method in composing his dramas can be demonstrated from a comparison of the earlier

---

[1] On the other hand it has been pointed out that his knowledge of Greek was negligible. He makes many mistakes in *Penthesilea*, e.g. he believes that the Eumenides were the gate-keepers of Hell.

and the later drafts of *Penthesilea*. The changes which he made indicate the intuitive, unpremeditated quality of his writing in conformity
with the principles he has stated in *Über die allmähliche Verfertigung der
Gedanken beim Reden*. Certain motifs and ideas lay dormant and
matured in his mind after the greater portion of the work had been
completed. They were introduced into the drama at a late stage and
they do not fuse harmoniously with the rest of the tragedy. Psycho-
logically and dramatically, however, they are of considerable
importance and they may be regarded as representing the dominant
theme of the completed work.

The most important alterations occur in the seventh, ninth, fifteenth, twentieth and twenty-fourth scenes of the play. They all serve
to illuminate the deeper causes of Penthesilea's tragedy: her love for
Achilles and the allegiance which she owes to the god Mars.

Penthesilea, the queen of the Amazons is bound by the law of
Tanais. This law demands that the queen and her subjects shall not
wed any man who has not been conquered in battle. At the command
of Mars, the protective deity of the Amazon state, a war is begun
against a nation selected by the god, and the men conquered in it
become the mates of their victors. These 'marriages' are celebrated
after the battle is over at the so-called 'Rosenfest.' Penthesilea
explains these customs to Achilles after the Amazons' sudden and
furious attack had for so long bewildered the Greeks and the Trojans
alike. Penthesilea also reports that her mother Otrere on her death-
bed had predicted that Achilles was to be her future mate:

> Sie sagte: 'geh, mein süsses Kind! Mars ruft dich!
> Du wirst den Peleïden dir bekränzen:
> Werd' eine Mutter, stolz und froh, wie ich — '
> Und drückte sanft die Hand mir, und verschied. [cxx].

This mention of a particular man is a breach of the laws governing
the Amazon state. Prothoe is surprised to hear of Otrere's indiscretion
and Penthesilea, admitting the mistake, explains it to Achilles:

> Es schickt sich nicht, dass eine Tochter Mars'
> Sich ihren Gegner sucht, den soll sie wählen,
> Den ihr der Gott im Kampf erscheinen lässt. — [cxxi].

These words are not found in the first draft of the play. Kleist added
them when he revised his work in 1808. They emphasize the fact that
one cause of Penthesilea's tragedy is her mother's infringement
of the Amazon law. This means that by mentioning Achilles she has

deprived the god of his prerogative and has induced Penthesilea to centre her thoughts upon one individual, one particular man, thus violating the spirit of the law which governs the Amazons' choice of their husbands. Love in the usual meaning of the word is denied them. The very existence of their state depends upon the strict observance of the law of impersonal love. Penthesilea describes the effects of Otrere's indiscretion:

> Ich dachte so: wenn sie sich allzusamt,
> Die grossen Augenblicke der Geschichte,
> Mir wiederholten, wenn die ganze Schar
> Der Helden, die die hohen Lieder feiern,
> Herab mir aus den Sternen stieg', ich fände
> Doch keinen Trefflichern, den ich mit Rosen
> Bekränzt', als ihn, den mir die Mutter ausersehn —
> Den Lieben, Wilden, Süssen, Schrecklichen,
> Den Überwinder Hektors! O Pelide!
> Mein ewiger Gedanke, wenn ich wachte,
> Mein ew'ger Traum warst du! Die ganze Welt
> Lag wie ein ausgespanntes Musternetz
> Vor mir; in jeder Masche, weit und gross,
> War deiner Taten eine eingeschürzt,
> Und in mein Herz, wie Seide weiss und rein,
> Mit Flammenfarben jede brannt' ich ein. [cxxii].

On her way to Troy her thoughts dwelt upon his image. When she saw him for the first time her admiration for him grew into love:

> Im Augenblick, Pelid', erriet ich es,
> Von wo mir das Gefühl zum Busen rauschte;
> Der Gott der Liebe hatte mich ereilt. [cxxiii].

In the original version Penthesilea had described the growth of her love with the simple words: 'Mein ewiger Traum warst du!' Kleist inserted the elaborate metaphor depicting her preoccupation with the image of Achilles in order to emphasize her infatuation.

In those portions of the play where the other Amazons discuss Penthesilea's love for Achilles, Kleist again revised his text with a view to accentuating the motif of her guilt.

After the Amazons had won their initial victory and captured a sufficient number of Greeks to enable them to celebrate the Feast of the Roses and return to Themiscyra, Penthesilea begins the battle again in order to capture Achilles. Her resolve comes as a surprise to her followers and Prothoe incurs her anger by attempting to restrain her from yielding to her passion (Scene 5). When the progress of the battle is reported, the High Priestess severely condemn the conduct of the queen and her love for Achilles, and predicts her downfall:

> *Die Hauptmännin* Jedwede Kunst der Rede ward erschöpft,
> Nach Themiscyra sie zurückzuführen.
> Doch taub schien sie der Stimme der Vernunft:
> Vom giftigsten der Pfeile Amors sei,
> Heisst es, ihr jugendliches Herz getroffen.
>
> . . . .
>
> *Die Oberpriesterin* (zur Hauptmännin)
> Die Königin, sagst du? Unmöglich, Freundin!
> Von Amors Pfeil getroffen — wann? Und wo?
> Die Führerin des Diamantengürtels?
> Die Tochter Mars', der selbst der Busen fehlt,
> Das Ziel der giftgefiederten Geschosse?
> *Die Hauptmännin* So sagt des Volkes Stimme mindestens,
> Und Meroe hat es eben mir vertraut.
> *Die Oberpriesterin* Es ist entsetzlich!
>
> . . . .
>
> O sie geht steil-bergab den Pfad zum Orkus!
> Und nicht dem Gegner, wenn sie auf ihn trifft,
> Dem Feind' in ihrem Busen wird sie sinken. [cxxiv].

This dialogue is not found in the earlier draft of the drama. Kleist made the addition for the purpose of giving a clearer motivation of Penthesilea's tragedy. The same object is served by the following passage from the ninth scene:

> *Prothoe*   Geht, ihr Jungfraun,
> Geht; kehrt in eure Heimatsflur zurück:
> Die Königin und ich, wir bleiben hier.
> *Die Oberpriesterin* Wie, du Unsel'ge? Du bestärkst sie noch?
> *Meroe* Unmöglich wär's ihr, zu entfliehn?
> *Die Oberpriesterin*   Unmöglich,
> Da nichts von aussen sie, kein Schicksal, hält,
> Nichts als ihr töricht Herz —
> *Prothoe*   Das ist ihr Schicksal!
> Dir scheinen Eisenbanden unzerreissbar,
> Nicht wahr? Nun sieh: sie bräche sie vielleicht,
> Und das Gefühl doch nicht, das du verspottest.
> Was in ihr walten mag, das weiss nur sie,
> Und jeder Busen ist, der fühlt, ein Rätsel. [cxxv].

Among the Amazons the High Priestess consistently represents the interests of the state and therefore she is Penthesilea's harshest judge. Prothoe, on the other hand, is the queen's most sympathetic follower and her verdicts are inspired by her desire to understand and to condone Penthesilea's conduct. In the concluding lines of the play she assesses the cause of Penthesilea's tragedy:

> Sie sank, weil sie zu stolz und kräftig blühte!
> Die abgestorbne Eiche steht im Sturm,
> Doch die gesunde stürzt er schmetternd nieder,
> Weil er in ihre Krone greifen kann. [cxxvi].

The High Priestess had said that Penthesilea was rushing to her doom because she was not sustained from without, because her feelings swept her away:

> Da nichts von aussen sie, kein Schicksal, hält,
> Nichts als ihr töricht Herz —

Prothoe had defended the queen with the plea that feelings are mightier than bonds of iron. Now, after Penthesilea has died, she realizes that another force had hastened the calamity. Penthesilea succumbs to a stronger power outside herself. She is borne down by a storm and she falls not in spite of, but because of her inward strength.

This is a salient feature of her tragic fate. It is of great importance for assessing the meaning of Kleist's last tragedy, and likewise for an understanding of his later dramas. He paid much attention to this aspect of *Penthesilea* when he produced the revised version in 1808. The external motivation of the tragedy is hardly prominent in the first draft of the work. It becomes an essential part of the action in the finished product. By modifying the text of some passages and by inserting others, Kleist worked into his play the theme of Penthesilea's conflict against a superior external power, just as he accentuated her guilt in other portions of the drama.

In a letter to Wilhelmine von Zenge on November 16, 1800 he gives the following description of an experience which he had in Würzburg: 'Ich ging an jenem Abend vor dem wichtigsten Tage meines Lebens in Würzburg spazieren. Als die Sonne herabsank war es mir als ob mein Glück unterginge. Mich schauerte wenn ich dachte, dass ich vielleicht von Allem scheiden müsste, von Allem, was mir teuer ist. Da ging ich, in mich gekehrt, durch das gewölbte Tor sinnend zurück in die Stadt. Warum, dachte ich, sinkt wohl das Gewölbe nicht ein, da es doch keine Stütze hat? Es steht, antwortete ich, weil alle Steine auf einmal einstürzen wollen — und ich zog aus

diesem Gedanken einen unbeschreiblich erquickenden Trost . . .'
[cxxvii]. The vault symbolized the precariousness as well as the
inherent strength of life, and Kleist often used this image to describe
the paradox of human existence. In the first draft of *Penthesilea* it
occurs in Prothoe's exhortation to the queen:

> Komm' meine Königin! Erhebe dich!
> Du wirst in diesem Augenblick nicht sinken.
> Oft wenn im Menschen Alles untergeht,
> So hält ihn dies: wie das Gewölbe steht,
> Weil seiner Blöcke jeder stürzen will. [cxxviii].

In the final version we find this image in a greatly modified form;
Kleist has altered it in such a way that it now contains a new thought.
It is a good example of his method of extracting significant values
from every detail of the picture which he employs:

> So hebst du dich empor? — Nun, meine Fürstin,
> So sei's auch wie ein Riese! Sinke nicht,
> Und wenn der ganze Orkus auf dich drückte!
> Steh, stehe fest, wie das Gewölbe steht,
> Weil seiner Blöcke jeder stürzen will!
> Beut deine Scheitel, einem Schlussstein gleich,
> Der Götter Blitzen dar, und rufe: trefft!
> Und lass dich bis zum Fuss herab zerspalten,
> Nicht aber wanke in dir selber mehr,
> Solang' ein Atem Mörtel und Gestein
> In dieser jungen Brust, zusammenhält. [cxxix].

The simile of the first version has become a metaphor conveying a
new meaning, which is contained in Prothoe's exhortation to
Penthesilea to defy the gods who have struck her down. The power
which threatens destruction to the queen is not, as the High Priestess
had maintained, the inward force of passion, but the angry violence
of the gods. Prothoe knows at the end that the tempest has destroyed
Penthesilea and the queen herself feels that she is the victim of divine
displeasure. In the last scene of the play, when the body of Achilles
is carried in, as yet unaware of her gruesome deed, but sensing
disaster, she blames the gods for human failures:

> Zwar einer Schwalbe Flügel kann ich lähmen,
> So, dass der Flügel noch zu heilen ist;
> Den Hirsch lock' ich mit Pfeilen in den Park.
> Doch ein Verräter ist die Kunst der Schützen;
> Und gilt's den Meisterschuss ins Herz des Glückes,
> So führen tück'sche Götter uns die Hand. [cxxx].

The last two lines are not found in the first draft, but were added in the final version of the play, again revealing Kleist's later preoccupation with the theme of divine intervention in the action of his play. In the light of this theme the addition of the following lines, which have already been mentioned, in Scene 1, 15, is particularly significant:

> Es schickt sich nicht, dass eine Tochter Mars'
> Sich ihren Gegner sucht, den soll sie wählen,
> Den ihr der Gott im Kampf erscheinen lässt. [cxxxi].

In revising his text Kleist gave prominence to Mars' relationship with the Amazons, especially with Penthesilea, which previously he had not stressed. It becomes a cardinal factor in the motivation of Penthesilea's tragedy.

Among the authorities whom Kleist may have consulted on the legend of Penthesilea, some accepted the belief that the Amazons descended from Mars, while others refuted this view. To the latter belonged the Abbé Guyon. In his *Histoire des Amazons* (1740) he writes: 'Il est contre toute vraisemblance qu'aucune d'elles se soit donnée pour fille et pour femme du Dieu Mars.'[1] Zedler, on the other hand, states in the article 'Amazonen': 'Ihr Geschlechte führten sie von dem Marte her . . ., einige aber geben sie insonderheit vor die Töchter des Martis und der Harmoniae, einer Najade, aus . . . Hingegen halten andre nur einige von denselben vor die Töchter besagten Gottes.' [cxxxii]. In the article 'Penthesilea' he says that Penthesilea was 'the daughter of Mars and Otrere.'[2] Kleist utilized this view rather than that of Guyon and the more he worked at the drama, the more he emphasized it. When Penthesilea gives Achilles an account of the Amazon state, she dwells upon the part which Mars had played at its inauguration. He had consummated the marriage that had been arranged between Vexoris and the founder of the Amazon state Tanais, after she had killed the usurping king. Since then the influence of Mars had remained paramount. He chose the people which the Amazons were to conquer to propagate their kind:

> Der Gott zeigt uns, durch seine Priesterin,
> Ein Volk an, keusch und herrlich, das, statt seiner,
> Als Stellvertreter, uns erscheinen soll. [cxxxiii].

These nations are called his 'Representatives' because he guides the

---

[1] Part II, p. 161.
[2] *Grosses Universal Lexicon aller Wissenschaften und Künste*, 1732–1750. Vols. I, col. 1667, and XXVII. col. 289.

F

Amazons in battle and presides over their marriage celebrations at
the Feast of the Roses, a circumstance which explains the High
Priestess' irate command to the recalcitrant Penthesilea:

> Fleuch gleich, Arsinoe, vor ihr Antlitz hin,
> Und sag' in meiner Göttin Namen ihr,
> Mars habe seinen Bräuten sich gestellt:
> Ich forderte, bei ihrem Zorn, sie auf,
> Den Gott bekränzt zur Heimat jetzt zu führen,
> Und unverzüglich ihm, in ihrem Tempel,
> Das heil'ge Fest der Rosen zu eröffnen. [cxxxiv].

This formulation is much more expressive than that of the earlier
version:

> Und sag' ihr: Mars, ihr grosser Ahnherr, habe
> Des Volkes Wunsch erhört, ich forderte,
> Der Diana hohe Oberpriesterin,
> Zur Rückkehr in die Heimat sie, verzuglos
> Zur Feier jetzt des Rosenfestes auf![1]

In addition to his tutelary connection with the Amazons' affairs,
Mars had a particular place in Penthesilea's life. She gives Achilles
the following account:

> Sieh, ich hatte schon
> Das heitre Fest der Rosen zwanzigmal
> Erlebt und drei, und immer nur von fern,
> Wo aus dem Eichenwald der Tempel ragt,
> Den frohen Jubelschall gehört, als Ares
> Bei der Otrere, meiner Mutter, Tod
> Zu seiner Braut mich auserkor. Denn die
> Prinzessinnen, aus meinem Königshaus,
> Sie mischen nie, aus eigener Bewegung,
> Sich in der blühnden Jungfrau'n Fest; der Gott,
> Begehrt er ihrer, ruft sie würdig auf,
> Durch seiner grossen Oberpriestrin Mund.
> Die Mutter lag, die bleiche, scheidende,
> Mir in den Armen eben, als die Sendung
> Des Mars mir feierlich im Palast erschien,
> Und mich berief, nach Troja aufzubrechen,
> Um ihn von dort bekränzt heranzuführen. [cxxxv].

---

[1] These passages also show that there is much confusion in the play about the relative positions
of Diana and Mars in the Amazon state. She is the goddess whom the High Priestess serves,
but it is not clear whether her authority is equal to that of Mars. Artemis and Mars are
mentioned in different legends about the Amazons. Kleist has used both traditions without
attempting to reconcile them in his play.

The peculiarity of Penthesilea's position becomes clearer when we remember an earlier passage in her account:

> So oft, nach jährlichen Berechnungen,
> Die Königin, was ihr der Tod entrafft,
> Dem Staat ersetzen will, ruft sie die blühndsten
> Der Frau'n, von allen Enden ihres Reichs,
> Nach Themiscyra hin, und fleht, im Tempel
> Der Artemis, auf ihre jungen Schösse
> Den Segen keuscher Marsbefruchtung nieder. [cxxxvi].

This explanation is somewhat obscure, but it does illuminate the difference between Penthesilea's mission and the functions of more ordinary Amazons. While the queen chooses the women for child-bearing, the queen herself awaits the call of Mars. This circumstance, then, would indicate that Penthesilea's guilt is primarily a betrayal of her duty towards Mars. She says herself that after Otrere had told her to seek out Achilles, she went forth to Troy

> Mars weniger,
> Dem grossen Gott, der mich dahin gerufen,
> Als der Otrere Schatten, zu gefallen [cxxxvii].

and thus her feeling when she meets Achilles for the first time acquires a peculiar significance:

> So müsst'es mir gewesen sein, wenn er
> Unmittelbar, mit seinen weissen Rossen,
> Von dem Olymp herabgedonnert wäre,
> Mars selbst, der Kriegsgott, seine Braut zu grüssen! [cxxxviii].

We now understand the implications of her admission: 'Der Gott der Liebe hatte mich ereilt' and the High Priestess' horror when she hears about Penthesilea's love.

The action of the drama becomes intelligible only if we assume that Mars, angered by Penthesilea's defection, intervenes in order to hamper her exploit. When she pursues Achilles on horse-back she is suddenly and unaccountably overcome by weakness:

> Drauf plötzlich jetzt legt sie die Zügel weg:
> Man sieht, gleich einer Schwindelnden, sie hastig
> Die Stirn, von einer Lockenflut umwallt,
> In ihre beiden kleinen Hände drücken.
> Bestürzt, bei diesem sonderbaren Anblick,
> Umwimmeln alle Jungfraun sie . . . [cxxxix].

The farther the action advances the more she appears to have been struck by the irate god. After her fall, described in Scene 3, she completely loses control over her mental and her emotional powers. She surprises her most intimate followers by the strange excess of her passion and she is bewildered when Prothoe advises her to postpone decisions until she is in a more serene mood:

> Warum? Weshalb? Was ist geschehn? Was sagt' ich?
> Hab' ich? — Was hab' ich denn — ? [cxl]. (Scene 5).

After Achilles has defeated her in single combat her moods become even more unpredictable and her derangement more frightening to her followers. In Scene 9, in two separate but connected instances, the Amazons are the perplexed witnesses of Penthesilea's frenzy; Achilles and Apollo seem to have become identified in her mind and her passionate desire to conquer the one is expressed in her mad yearning to lay low the other:

Penthesilea (die während dessen unverwandt in die Sonne gesehen):
  Dass ich mit Flügeln, weit gespreizt und rauschend,
  Die Luft zerteilte—!
Prothoe   Wie?
Meroe   Was sagte sie?
Prothoe   Was siehst du, Fürstin — ?
Meroe   Worauf heftet sich — ?
Prothoe   Geliebte, sprich!
Penthesilea   Zu hoch, ich weiss, zu hoch —
  Er spielt in ewig fernen Flammenkreisen
  Mir um den sehnsuchtsvollen Busen hin.

Penthesilea Eins noch, ihr Freundinnen, und rasend wär' ich,
  Das müsst' ihr selbst gestehn, wenn ich im ganzen
  Gebiet der Möglichkeit mich nicht versuchte.
Prothoe (unwillig): Nun denn, so wollt' ich, dass wir gleich versänken!
  Denn Rettung gibt's nicht mehr.
Penthesilea (erschrocken):   Was ist? Was fehlt dir?
  Was hab' ich ihr getan, ihr Jungfraun, sprecht!
Die Oberpriesterin Du denkst — ?
Meroe   Du willst auf diesem Platze noch — ?
Penthesilea Nichts, nichts, gar nichts, was sie erzürnen sollte. —
  Den Ida will ich auf den Ossa wälzen,
  Und auf die Spitze ruhig bloss mich stellen.
Die Oberpriesterin Den Ida wälzen — ?
Meroe   Wälzen auf den Ossa — ?
Prothoe (mit einer Wendung): Schützt, all' ihr Götter, sie!
Die Oberpriesterin   Verlorene!

Meroe (schüchtern): Dies Werk ist der Giganten, meine Königin!
Penthesilea Nun ja, nun ja: worin denn weich' ich ihnen?
Meroe   Worin du ihnen — ?
Prothoe   Himmel!
Die Oberpriesterin   Doch gesetzt — ?
Meroe   Gesetzt nun, du vollbrächtest dieses Werk — ?
Prothoe   Gesetzt, was würdest du — ?
Penthesilea   Blödsinnige!
      Bei seinen goldnen Flammenhaaren zög' ich
      Zu mir hernieder ihn —
Prothoe   Wen?
Penthesilea   Helios,
      Wenn er am Scheitel mir vorüberfleucht!
(Die Fürstinnen sehn sprachlos und mit Entsetzen einander an) [cxli].

These instances are good examples of Kleist's dramatic technique in presenting unexpected moments of extreme emotional tension or surprising developments of cardinal importance. A secret and irrational desire is dragged into the light of day by assaults of questions, reiterated phrases and exclamations and by insistent probing, and in this process of cross-examination the rhythmic structure of the language is preserved although it is broken into fragments of significant speech. Instances of this kind can be found in each of Kleist's dramas. They reveal the deeper mainsprings of the action and the ultimate source of the ensuing catastrophe.

Penthesilea's enigmatic outburts in the ninth scene, her identification of Apollo and Achilles, her preparations for the last battle in Scene 20 ('kniet nieder, mit allen Zeichen des Wahnsinns') [cxlii] and finally her gruesome revenge upon Achilles are the progressive symptoms of what Prothoe calls the eclipse of her mind ('des Verstandes Sonnenfinsternis') leading to the ultimate catastrophe. The true meaning of her frenzy is made clear again when the High Priestess warns her against incurring Mars' displeasure, an admonition which she defiantly rejects:

Die Oberpriesterin Hörst du ihn, Königin, der dir zürnt?
Penthesilea   Ihn ruf' ich
            Mit allen seinen Donnern mir herab! [cxliii].

Penthesilea's tragedy is Alkmene's tragedy in an intensified, a more radical form. In both dramas the heroine's 'Verwirrung des Gefühls' is the pivot of the psychological action. Since the confusion of Penthesilea's mind is caused by the god's displeasure, while Alkmene's is the result of a deceit practised upon her, and since the Amazon queen occupies a position in life which is characterized by its peculiar eminence as well as its singular limitations, she is exposed to dangers far greater than those that beset Alkmene and the results of her conflicts are much more disastrous. Madness, fury, perversion, carnage and death are the effects of Penthesilia's tragic infringement of the law of the Amazons.

She is aware of the fact of her transgression, but she appears not to have understood its true nature. In resolving to conquer Achilles she does not separate her love and her leadership in the war. Her conflict is not a collision between her inclinations as a woman and her duty as a queen. Her desire to win Achilles is indissolubly linked with the ambition to capture him in battle and she does not comprehend her followers when they accuse her of betraying the cause of the Amazons by refusing to desist from her purpose. She even believes that she has failed in her duty as their queen by allowing Achilles to escape:

> Nein, eh' ich, was so herrlich mir begonnen,
> So gross, nicht endige, eh' ich nicht völlig
> Den Kranz, der mir die Stirn umrauscht', erfasse,
> Eh' ich Mars' Töchter nicht, wie ich versprach,
> Jetzt auf des Glückes Gipfel jauchzend führe,
> Eh' möge seine Pyramide schmetternd
> Zusammenbrechen über mich und sie:
> Verflucht das Herz, das sich nicht mäss'gen kann. [cxliv]. (Scene 5).

The last line of this speech by Penthesilea has given rise to some misunderstanding. It has been taken to signify an appeal for moderation on the part of the queen herself, but this would contradict the spirit of her whole speech and of her entire attitude from her first meeting with Achilles onwards. Penthesilea is, indeed, arguing not for the restraint but for the release of her passion. 'If I do not conquer Achilles,' she says, 'let the ruin of our fortunes overtake us, and if that is what you wish to bring about, then you may curse the heart that cannot submit to moderation.' Kleist, with great effect, uses rhetorical devices such as the hiatus and the anacoluthon in order to portray the emotional distress of his characters.

In addition to the infringement of the law of Tanais, Penthesilea's guilt is caused by her inability to curb her passionate desire to conquer Achilles, and her refusal to recognize her own intemperance:

> Ist's meine Schuld, dass ich im Feld der Schlacht
> Um sein Gefühl mich kämpfend muss bewerben?
> Was will ich denn, wenn ich das Schwert ihm zücke?
> Will ich ihn denn zum Orkus niederschleudern?
> Ich will ihn ja, ihr ew'gen Götter, nur
> An diese Brust will ich ihn niederziehn. [cxlv].

Implicit in these words is a criticism of the status of Amazon women, and the final scene of the drama will reveal Penthesilea's attitude more clearly. Before her last encounter with Achilles, however, she does not outspokenly dissociate herself from the laws of the state. When she eventually breaks away from its established order, her tragedy has already reached its culmination. The climax of her conflict is the realization, not of the incompatibility of her duty with her desire, but of her failure to achieve her desire, to win Achilles by force of arms. This conflict begins in the fifth scene of the drama and reaches the first summit in the fifteenth scene, and the second crisis in the nineteenth scene. In the fifteenth scene she is humiliated by the news that she had been conquered by Achilles and that she had been wrongly led to believe in her own supremacy. From this moment her attitude to him changes radically. His ruthless behaviour when the Amazons approach to liberate her fills her with dismay, but she accepts the rigours of the war in which she is personally engaged, the war of love with Achilles, and spurns the victory of her followers which has set her free:

> Verflucht sei dieser schändliche Triumph mir!
>
> . . . .
>
> Gibt's ein Gesetz, frag' ich, in solchem Kriege,
> Das den Gefangenen, der sich ergeben,
> Aus seines Siegers Banden lösen kann? [cxlvi]. (Scene 19).

Her love for Achilles has not yet been shattered, but she is overwhelmed by shame when the High Priestess reproaches her for throwing away the victory that had been gained by the Amazons and demands the cessation of hostilities. Penthesilea's mood has now changed from sorrow over her personal defeat to despair over the adversity which she has brought upon her army. Finally it swings back to a sense of her own humiliation, for when she receives Achilles' challenge to another combat, she believes that he has spurned her love and is seeking to degrade her, that the kindness he had shown towards her had merely been pity for her physical distress:

> Hier diese Brust, sie rührt ihn erst,
> Wenn sie sein scharfer Speer zerschmetterte?
> Was ich ihm zugeflüstert, hat sein Ohr
> Mit der Musik der Rede bloss getroffen? [cxlvii].[1]

Her love turns to hate and she sets out to destroy Achilles despite the imprecations of her followers and the manifest disapproval of the god. She is blinded by the passion of revenge as Rupert is in *Die Familie Schroffenstein* and like him, when the deed is accomplished, not a trace of its memory remains. When Achilles meets her almost unarmed, she is too enraged to notice his pacific intentions. She kills him in a transport of fury and savagery, a debased form of the love which she still feels for him.

The alteration of Penthesilea's love into savage hate represents the climax of the tragedy and her slaughter of Achilles its catastrophe. Her awakening from the trance-like state in which she killed him, her repudiation of the laws of Tanais and her death, constitute its dénouement.

Penthesilea's tragedy has two causes: the excess of her passion and the displeasure of Mars; and it has two consequences: the destruction of the Amazon state and her own death. The first of these consequences is represented symbolically by the episode of the great bow, the emblem of the Amazon state. This bow is endowed with almost living power and human properties. In her account in the fifteenth scene Penthesilea describes the part it played at the foundation of the Amazon state. When Tanais had ascended the altar steps to receive the bow which the Scythian kings had wielded, a voice was heard to say that the new state could not survive because the women would not be able to defend it:

> 'Weil doch die Kraft des Bogens nimmermehr,
> Von schwachen Fraun, beengt durch volle Brüste,
> Leicht, wie von Männern, sich regieren würde.' [cxlviii].

Perceiving the effect which these words had on the assembled

---

[1] These words show, as does the action of the drama from Scene 15 onwards, that the themes of misunderstanding and error still play an important part in this tragedy. By comparison with *Die Familie Schroffenstein*, however, in *Penthesilea* they have lost some of their importance, since they are linked with, and subordinated to, the other themes treated in this work. The modification of Kleist's conception of tragedy from the time of its inception under the influence of Kant to its disappearance after the composition of *Penthesilea* is indicated by the subordination of the themes of error and misunderstanding in his last tragic work.

women, Tanais tore off her right breast and proceeded to baptize
the women who were eligible for combat. Then the bow behaved
in an extraordinary manner:

> Still auch auf diese Tat ward's, Peleïde,
> Nichts als der Bogen liess sich schwirrend hören,
> Der aus den Händen, leichenblass und starr,
> Der Oberpriesterin darniederfiel.
> Er stürzt', der grosse, goldene, des Reichs,
> Und klirrte von der Marmorstufe dreimal,
> Mit dem Gedröhn der Glocken, auf, und legte,
> Stumm wie der Tod zu ihren Füssen sich. — [cxlix].

This enigmatic passage suggests that the Scythians had been finally
vanquished by the Amazons. The last vestige of their power has
been surrendered to the women and submitted to their sway. Henceforth the bow became the symbol of Amazon might in the hands of
the queen. Penthesilea receives it when she sets out for Troy and she
uses it to slay Achilles. When she returns from the scene of the
carnage and awakens from her trance, she drops the bow and once
more it acts like a living being:

> *Die erste Amazone* Der Bogen stürzt' ihr aus der Hand danieder!
> *Die zweite* Seht, wie er taumelt —
> *Die vierte*   Klirrt und wankt und fällt!
> *Die zweite* Und noch einmal am Boden zuckt —
> *Die dritte*   Und stirbt,
> Wie er der Tanais geboren ward. [cl]

With the destruction of the bow, we may surmise, the power of the
Amazons has gone. In vain the High Priestess attempts to reassure
Penthesilea. She bids farewell to her followers and counsels the formal
dissolution of the Amazon state:

> Und — — — im Vertraun ein Wort, das niemand höre:
> Der Tanais Asche, streut sie in die Luft! [cli].

Her own death is an act of intense volition, a summoning of that
inward strength which Prothoe had believed in as a means to escape
the vengeance of the gods:

> Denn jetzt steig' ich in meinen Busen nieder,
> Gleich einem Schacht, und grabe, kalt wie Erz,
> Mir ein vernichtendes Gefühl hervor.
> Dies Erz, dies läutr' ich in der Glut des Jammers
> Hart mir zu Stahl; tränk' es mit Gift sodann,

Heissätzendem, der Reue, durch und durch;
Trag' es der Hoffnung ew'gem Amboss zu,
Und schärf' und spitz' es mir zu einem Dolch;
Und diesem Dolch jetzt reich' ich meine Brust:
So! So! So! So! Und wieder! — Nun ist's gut.
                       (Sie fällt und stirbt.) [clii].

In this passage Kleist again reveals his power of portraying emotional crises by means of imagery. Here we have an example of his use of allegory to this end. It has the same quality of succinctness and completeness which is found in his use of metaphors and symbols. Its cohesiveness is perhaps too logical, since it is dramatically improbable that Penthesilea, in her most dire distress, should be able to summon the powers of intellect and imagination enabling her to conceive and elaborate the picture describing her moral suicide. On the other hand it may be said that she has risen above the crisis, which is represented by her discovery of the true facts about Achilles' death, and thus is in a fit state of mind to employ her intellectual rather than her emotional powers. Viewed in this light her elaborate image may be regarded as a fine piece of dramatic portrayal and a characteristic example of Kleist's poetic art.

In his last and most uncompromising tragedy Kleist revealed the destructive power of the forces that rule human life—the internal compulsion of passion and the external coercion of divine authority.

When he began to write the drama he was apparently preoccupied with the first aspect of Penthesilea's tragedy and did not consider the second so fully. In the first draft of his work the motivation of the action rests almost entirely on the overweening strength of her passion. For the treatment of this theme the form which he chose, the continuous series of scenes that he had successfully used in *Der Zerbrochene Krug* proved entirely suitable. When Kleist changed the whole character of his tragedy by duplicating the motivation, he left the form unaltered. Many of the difficulties that have been experienced in the interpretation of *Penthesilea* arise from the fact that this technique does not adequately represent both aspects of the dramatic action, the outward as well as the inward causes of Penthesilea's downfall. Penthesilea's inner conflict alone, particularly from the fifth to the nineteenth scenes, has determined the shape of the work. A balanced form entailing a division into Acts with due regard for the distribution of the different forces influencing the course of the action would more successfully reflect the total impression which

Kleist intended to convey in the finished version of the tragedy. Despite this drawback, however, *Penthesilea* remains his most characteristic and his most representative tragic production. It embraces all the aspects of tragedy which his analysis of human life suggested to him and it fully reveals his mastery in the creation and in the presentation, both directly and through the extensive use of images and symbols, of singularly powerful dramatic situations.

V

DAS KÄTHCHEN VON HEILBRONN AND DIE HERMANNSSCHLACHT

THERE is some evidence for believing that Kleist was influenced by G. H. Schubert's *Nachtseite der Naturwissenschaft* when he wrote *Penthesilea*. Here he was introduced to the problem of dual personality and of those darker sides of human nature which the writers and philosophers of the eighteenth century, including Kant, had ignored. Schubert quotes the case of a pregnant woman who is seized by a violent desire to slay her husband, whom she dearly loves, and to eat his flesh.[1]

This affinity between 'Wollust' and 'Mordlust' is exemplified in *Penthesilea*, but it is not the most important theme of the tragedy and Kleist's indebtedness to Schubert should not be exaggerated. His next drama, *Das Käthchen von Heilbronn*, similarly shows traces of Schubert's influence, but again this is true only of one aspect of the work. Kleist utilized the Romantic valuation of instinct and intuition as being superior to reason or passion, and he borrowed other ideas which the Romantics had made popular, but his drama is not merely a collection of borrowed material. It bears the imprint of his peculiar genius although he recognized himself that he had made concessions to the taste of the age. 'Das Urteil der Menschen' he wrote in a letter in August 1811 'hat mich bisher viel zu sehr beherrscht; besonders das Käthchen von Heilbronn ist voll Spuren davon. Es war von Anfang herein eine ganz treffliche Erfindung, und nur die Absicht, es für die Bühne passend zu machen, hat mich zu Missgriffen verführt, die ich jetzt beweinen möchte.' [cliii].

It is possible to account for a large number of Kleist's borrowings by comparing his play with the dramatized fairy stories and tales in the 'Gothic' manner, which flourished in Germany at the end of the eighteenth century. From the stock incidents and motifs of these productions he took the secret trial ('Vehmgericht') with which he opens the play, the tempests, the duels, the assaults upon castles, the scene in the charcoal burner's hut, the abduction, and the character

[1] Cf. R. Tymms: *Alteration of Personality in Kleist and Werner, Modern Language Review*, Vol. XXXVII.

of Kunigunde who has a fatal attraction for men and who poisons her rivals and cast-off lovers.

The fairy tales from which he borrowed belong to one particular type, containing the theme of the two brides ('echte und falsche Braut'). They tell the story of a prince who is betrothed to a girl of humble origin, and who goes away and, forgetting about her, becomes engaged to somebody else. The girl follows him, lives near him in a humble position and on the wedding day is recognized and married by him.

Other borrowings are of a different kind. They concern the supernatural world and the world of occult phenomena, particularly the belief in astral bodies which is not frequently found in fairy tales. The visions of Wetter vom Strahl and Käthchen, their pre-ordained love, the appearance of the Cherub and the separation of Wetter vom Strahl's body and soul during an illness, are themes of this kind. It has been found possible to trace all these elements in the work of writers well-known to Kleist, e.g. Tieck and Wieland,[1] and it may be assumed that he had them in mind when he composed his play.

According to the taste of the critics *Käthchen von Heilbronn* has been condemned as patchwork or commended for its popular appeal. Clearly the character of the work is very different from that of Kleist's previous dramas. At first sight it appears to have little in common with his earlier productions. In this world of make-believe necessity has ceased to rule and, it might be said, his personal fears and aspirations, the mainsprings of his earlier work, both comic and tragic, have been held in suspense. It is, in such a view, a play written purely for the entertainment of the reader or the spectator, and no deeper meaning need be sought in it.

We must, however, consider several factors that relate to the composition of *Käthchen von Heilbronn*. They throw light on Kleist's profounder intentions and assist us in the interpretation of the play. Bülow gives the following report of a conversation between Kleist and Tieck: 'Nachdem Kleist das Käthchen von Heilbronn geschrieben, und Tieck mitgetheilt hatte, sprachen und stritten sie mannigfach darüber und sagte Tieck ihm unter anderen eine Meinung über eine merkwürdige Szene, die das ganze Stück gewissermassen in das Gebiet des Märchens oder Zaubers hinüberspielte. Kleist missverstand diese Äusserung als Tadel, vernichtete die Szene, ohne dass

[1] Cf. S.Wukadinović: *Über Kleists Käthchen von Heilbronn. Euphorion*, Vol. II, *Ergänzungsheft*, 1895, pp. 14–36, and F. Röbbeling: *Kleists Käthchen von Heilbronn, Bausteine zur Geschichte der neueren deutschen Literatur*, ed. F. Saran, 1913, pp. 73–107.

Tieck eine Ahnung davon hatte, und als dieser sie in der Folge im Druck vermisste, konnte er nicht aufhören, darüber sein Bedauern auszusprechen, weil sie die karikirte Hässlichkeit Kunigundens weit besser motivirt und sie in ein besseres Licht gerückt habe. Dieser Szene gemäss wandelte Käthchen im vierten Akt auf dem Felsen und erschien ihr unten im Wasser eine Nixe, die sie mit Gesang und Rede lockte. Käthchen wollte sich herabstürzen, und wurde nur durch eine Begleiterin gerettet. Vorher belauschte sie Kunigundens badende Hässlichkeit und war ausser sich vor Angst, wie sie den Ritter vor dem Ungeheuer errette.'[1] [cliv].

Several critics have thrown doubt upon Bülow's report, since Tieck does not mention the matter in any of his reminiscences. But this is merely an argument *a silentio*, and no stronger evidence has been adduced to disprove the account. We may, therefore, assume that in an earlier version of the play Kunigunde was not an ordinary woman, but a water-sprite, and that one of the sources of the drama was an adaptation of the well-known legend *Die schöne Melusine*. According to Kleist's earliest conception Kunigunde used her supernatural powers in her attempt to destroy Käthchen and she had a more sinister influence over Wetter vom Strahl and Käthchen than she now possesses. Some support for the view that Kleist curtailed the importance of Kunigunde in the later version is forthcoming when we compare the work in its present form with the fragment (Acts I and II) which Kleist published in 1808 in *Phöbus*, but which is a later text than the draft referred to in Bülow's report. A comparison of the version of 1808 with the final one will illuminate other important aspects of the drama.

In Act II, Scene 9, of the *Phöbus* draft, Kunigunde has a long conversation with Rosalie initiating her into the mysteries of her toilet. Her explanation is curiously reminiscent of Kleist's own views on art as he stated them in *Brief eines Dichters an einen anderen*, and it is out of keeping with her character. Kleist omitted it completely in the final version, probably for this reason, and because it was not compatible with a scene which he added after the publication of the *Phöbus* draft. Scene nine of this draft corresponds to the tenth scene of the complete work, in which he inserted the present ninth scene. In this scene Brigitte gives Kunigunde an account of Wetter vom Strahl's illness and his vision on the night when, as we learn later, Käthchen had her vision.

The events of that New Year's Eve, the unusual circumstances in

---

[1] *Heinrich von Kleists Leben und Briefe*, 1848, p. 56.

which Käthchen and Strahl first met each other, are of the greatest importance for the dramatic action. Käthchen's noble birth and these events together form the secret which, like Peter's death in *Die Familie Schroffenstein*, Jupiter's identity in *Amphitryon* and the reasons for the Amazons' attack upon the Greeks in *Penthesilea*, produces the complications that constitute a major portion of the action. The secret of Käthchen's origin is revealed only at the end of the play. The incident that took place on New Year's Eve, on the other hand, is disclosed at a time when Kunigunde can avail herself of the information to further her own plans.

The full meaning of Wetter vom Strahl's astral adventure does not become clear to us until Käthchen gives an account of her own experiences on the same night. This occurs in Act IV, Scene 2. Her story explains to us, as it does to Wetter vom Strahl, that his adventure is only one half of a larger design. It sheds a new light on the intricate relationship between Käthchen and Strahl and it brings with it a possible solution of the dramatic complications. The action of the play is virtually over at this point. The remainder of Act IV and the whole of Act V are merely a lengthy dénouement in which the disclosure of Käthchen's birth forms the last link. This final development, the discovery of Käthchen's lineage, has been criticized as a piece of snobbery, but it occupies an important place in the pattern of the whole drama. Brigitte tells Kunigunde that Wetter vom Strahl had been informed by the angel who accompanied him on his New Year's Eve expedition, that the girl he had seen was a daughter of the Emperor. His relations with Kunigunde and Käthchen are decisively influenced by this information. It enables Kunigunde to pose as the lady of Imperial Saxon birth and it motivates his harsh treatment of Käthchen even when he realizes that he loves her:

O du — — — wie nenn' ich dich? Käthchen! Warum kann ich dich nicht mein nennen? Käthchen, Mädchen, Käthchen! Warum kann ich dich nicht mein nennen? . . . Ihr grauen, bärtigen Alten, was wollt ihr? Warum verlasst ihr eure goldnen Rahmen, ihr Bilder meiner geharnischten Väter, die meinen Rüstsaal bevölkern, und tretet in unruhiger Versammlung hier um mich herum, eure ehrwürdigen Locken schüttelnd? Nein, nein, nein! Zum Weibe, wenn ich sie gleich liebe, begehr' ich sie nicht; eurem stolzen Reigen will ich mich anschliessen: das war beschlossne Sache, noch ehe ihr kamt. [clv]. (Act II, Scene 1).

If Käthchen had not been proved to be of Imperial Saxon stock, a vital thread of the action would have been left loose. The secrets of New Year's Eve and of Käthchen's birth are intimately linked together and the meaning of the drama is bound up with both of them.

Now if it can be assumed that in the earliest draft of the work Wetter vom Strahl's adventure did not exist and therefore that the present Scene 9 of the Second Act is not to be found in the *Phöbus* fragment because it did not belong to Kleist's earliest conception of the drama, then the true character of the play in its final form can be understood. It is possible that the whole episode of the New Year's Eve was added only after the publication of the first two Acts in 1808. This cannot be proved conclusively, since Käthchen's experience on that night is not made known until we reach the fourth Act. But since in the completed work Act II Scene 9 and Act IV Scene 2 are complementary to one another, it is reasonable to assume that the latter scene did not exist in a drama which does not contain the former.

If this hypothesis is correct, then it is obvious that the whole theme of divine predestination did not belong to Kleist's earliest conception of *Käthchen von Heilbronn*. In this connection it is significant that the theatre bill announcing the performance of the play on the stage at Vienna in 1810, did not contain the item 'der Kaiser' which now figures in the cast. Instead, a 'Herzog von Schwaben' heads the list of characters. It has been argued that this omission was due to censorship regulations, but it is more probable that the Emperor was not mentioned in the cast because he did not belong to it and because the whole complex of developments surrounding the theme of God's dispensation was a later addition to the drama. If this is true, then Kleist repeated the procedure which he had adopted in the writing of *Penthesilea*. When he revised his play for publication in its entirety he worked into it the crucial theme of the divine influence in the affairs of man.

The character of the earlier work was therefore quite different from that of the present drama. Remembering Bülow's report we can say that the only supernatural element in the original play was the evil power vested in Kunigunde. How much influence she exerted over Käthchen and Strahl is a matter for conjecture, but the similarity between the situation in *Penthesilea* and that of the earlier *Käthchen von Heilbronn* is most striking. The relationship of Strahl and Käthchen in the completed work is fraught with danger; in the first draft this potentiality of tragedy was almost certainly much greater. Now the overruling influence of divine Providence assures the happy solution of the complications. It is, however, a tragedy by contrast, since this happy solution appears to be a possibility only in the realm of the fairy-tale.

Owing to lack of reliable evidence it is impossible to state the reasons that prompted Kleist to make such a radical change in his drama. He may have been influenced by the writings or the lectures of Schubert and other Romantics, so that his whole outlook on life was altered, or he may have simply made a concession to popular taste in order to win some recognition as a dramatist. Perhaps his recession from pessimism was really the result of a natural reaction, a product of the innate tendencies of his spirit, not of external influences. Whatever the reasons were, he was able, for the first time in his literary career, to present an instance of the divine intervention in human life which did not lead to a tragic confusion of human relationships, but to their triumphant fruition.

In the completed drama Kunigunde is merely a base-willed, unscrupulous woman. She has been deprived of her supernatural powers and she now resorts to human devices of deception and assassination. Adelheid, in Goethe's *Götz von Berlichingen*, her literary ancestress, possessed real beauty. Kunigunde's beauty is not even skin-deep. In reality she is a pockmarked hag, a caricature of ugliness, as Tieck is reported to have put it. Only through her prowess at the toilet-table can she deceive men into believing her beautiful, and only by accident does Wetter vom Strahl discover the reality beneath the appearance. Kleist's tragic theme of human fallibility and the deceptiveness of appearances re-echoes distortedly in *Käthchen von Heilbronn*, just as the word 'Gefühl' which represents a high value in his previous work, occurs here in a debased form when Kunigunde uses it:

> Es sei. Es soll mir das Gefühl, das hier
> In diesem Busen sich entflammt, nicht stören.

> Ich will, dass dem Gefühl, das mir entflammt
> Im Busen ist, nichts fürder widerspreche! [clvi].

There are two principal conflicts in *Käthchen von Heilbronn*: first, the conflict of Wetter vom Strahl with Kunigunde, upon whose imposture a great deal of the outer action depends; and secondly, the conflict between him and Käthchen which is of a spiritual quality, although it sometimes takes the form of physical violence. These human collisions are under the control of Providence. The same Cherub conducts Strahl to Käthchen's chamber on the New Year's Eve and saves her from Kunigunde's murderous plots against her life. The

G

whole action of the play consists in the unfolding of a divine plan and the moral, if any, is expressed by the misguided Theobald who has done so much to thwart the predestined union of the lovers:

Was Gott fügt, heisst es, soll der Mensch nicht scheiden. [clvii].
(Act V, Scene 11).

In her obedience to the divine will Käthchen is more steadfast than Wetter vom Strahl. She acts with the certainty born of unconscious knowledge. She is as ignorant of the divine plan and of her own ancestry as Wetter vom Strahl, and she never thinks of him as her future lover. Her modesty and her humility are the result of her complete surrender to something she does not understand. It is a sign of grace. She is in the hands of a superior power and she does not oppose to it any will of her own. She is 'antigrav' in the sense of the word which Kleist uses in his essay *Über das Marionettentheater*, a puppet moving gracefully to the touch of the guiding fingers, an idealized figure in an unreal world, which also harbours the extravagant caricature of Kunigunde.

Kleist was not at his best when he tried his hand at this kind of drama. He lacks the poetic power to induce a suspension of our disbelief. The indiscriminate mixture of verse and prose which he employed for the only time (except for the unpublished *Die Familie Ghonorez*) in *Das Käthchen von Heilbronn* is another feature of an experiment that has not proved successful. In his next drama he attempted another experiment. He abandoned the realm of fancy for the world of political reality.

While *Die Hermannsschlacht* contains several themes that are found in Kleist's earlier work, it differs in its conception and its execution from all his previous dramas. He wrote it between May and December 1808 and intended that it should be performed in Vienna, where a campaign against France was in preparation. The motifs common to all his plays assume a new significance in this drama which is in effect a disguised appeal to the Germans to rise up against Napoleon under the combined leadership of the Austrian Emperor and the King of Prussia. The political situation in the year 1808 offered him an opportunity of utilizing his customary themes in a novel manner.

The dramatic action of *Die Hermannsschlacht* consists in the disclosure and the accomplishment of a secret enterprise: Hermann's plan to oust the Romans from German soil. This plan resembles the secrets which we find in *Robert Guiskard* and *Der Zerbrochene Krug* more closely than those of *Die Familie Schroffenstein* and *Käthchen von Heilbronn*, since it is not a hidden circumstance unknown to protagonists and antagonists alike, but a project in the mind of the principal character. There is, however, a striking difference between Guiskard's and Adam's mystification on the one hand and Hermann's secretiveness on the other hand. They attempt to conceal an unfortunate event that has already occurred, while it is his aim to put a plan into practical effect. His efforts are directed towards the realization of a future contingency, and he is actuated by motives of public, not merely of private interest. This scheme entailing the progressive accomplishment of a set purpose imposed new demands on Kleist's dramatic technique. *Die Hermannsschlacht* exhibits the 'stationäre Prozessform' only in a limited fashion and a more dynamic texture takes the place of the dialectical structure of the earlier dramas.

Kleist developed this new technique and yet, at the same time, adhered to his habitual principle of emphasizing states of mind rather than events of a physical character. In this drama he evolved the interesting method of presenting four separate but closely-knit parallel actions and one almost independent sub-plot. Hermann's relations with the four other important parties of the drama and Thusnelda's relations with Ventidius are the scattered yet well-co-ordinated centres of the dramatic interest.

Hermann's pursuit of his secret plan determines his attitude to the other four characters or groups of characters, to the German princes on his side of the river Weser, to Marbod on the other bank of the Weser, to his wife Thusnelda and to the Romans. In each case, except, for reasons of policy, in Marbod's case, he withholds his secret until the disclosure of his plans will assist the accomplishment of the aim for which he is working. Like other characters in Kleist's dramas he is a dissembler, but he is not primarily a deceiver. He never deceives Marbod and his dissimulation is a principle of his statecraft. The fact that Hermann fights for an ideal entirely changes the meaning of the theme of deception which Kleist had treated in some of his earlier dramas, notably in *Amphitryon*, *Der Zerbrochene Krug* and *Das Käthchen von Heilbronn*. *Die Hermannsschlacht* is the only work in which Kleist abandons his preoccupation with the lot of humanity in general and identifies himself with one section of it in opposition to another. His patriotism relegated his tragic perceptions to the back of his mind, just as his assumption of the efficacy of a benevolent Providence had done in *Das Käthchen von Heilbronn*.

Die Hermannsschlacht is a piece of propaganda. The note of actuality is apparent in the whole scheme of the work. While the main action more or less adheres to the facts as represented in the legend of Arminius' victory in the Teutoburger Wald, Kleist placed his emphasis in such a way that the parallel of the situation in his own day with the conditions under the Romans became obvious. He omitted the figure of Hermann's brother who ranks in the tradition as a supporter of Varus, and he introduced Marbod into the story of the German liberation. This had not been done by any of the writers who had dramatized the legend before Kleist. Marbod represents the Austrian Emperor and Kleist gave him a prominent share in the action, since it was Kleist's aim to promote the unification of Germany and Austria. He was an adherent of what, after 1848, was known as the 'Grossdeutsche Idee' which upheld this aim and was defeated by Bismarck's policy of uniting Germany under Prussian leadership. Kleist castigates German particularism in the episode of Aristan's treachery and expresses his political idea in the last scene when Hermann pays tribute to Marbod:

> Heil, Marbod, meinem edelmüt'gen Freund!
> Und wenn Germanien meine Stimme hört:
> Heil seinem grossen Oberherrn und König! [clviii].

The opinions and ambitions of the Romans in *Die Hermannsschlacht* represent Kleist's view of the Imperialist desires of France under Napoleon. They despise the Germans and their national aspirations and desire to dominate the world. In defence against them the adoption of any means whatsoever is permissible.

In his attitude to politics Kleist is a 'realist'. He is the first important political dramatist in modern German literature. Earlier writers had dramatized historical material containing political actions solely in order to present ethical problems, not to portray specifically political issues. *Die Hermannsschlacht* invites comparison with other works on the theme of national liberation, notably with J. E. Schlegel's *Hermann* drama, Klopstock's trilogy on Arminius, Goethe's *Egmont* and some of Schiller's plays. The difference between these works and Kleist's drama is largely a difference in political consciousness.

The poets of the eighteenth century in Germany regarded political activity mainly as a matter of cabals and intrigues and for this reason they looked upon it with suspicion. Schlegel's Hermann resists the temptation of partaking in such activity in order to preserve his honour and his integrity. Klopstock's hero can hardly be called a political, though he is a national, figure. Goethe had a keener sense of

the realities of politics, but it was far from his mind to use politics
in the drama for anything but purely dramatic reasons. The characters
of Egmont and Oranien were more important for him than their
political views. In *Fiesco* Schiller portrayed the tragedy of a man who
stoops to deception and intrigue in the cause of liberty. In *Don Carlos*
the practice of deceit is shown to bring about the frustration of the
noble cause which it was intended to serve, and the rebellion of the
Swiss in *Wilhelm Tell* is presented as an ideal revolution because the
laws of ethical conduct were carefully observed.

Kleist held another view. The observance of strictly ethical
standards was for him irrelevant as long as the aim of national liberation
was achieved. In *Die Hermannsschlacht* he plainly condones the practice of deceit if the situation demands it. When Hermann is told that
a Roman centurion had saved a child in Thuiskon at the risk of his
own life, he exclaims:

> Er sei verflucht, wenn er mir das getan!
> Er hat, auf einen Augenblick,
> Mein Herz veruntreut, zum Verräter
> An Deutschlands grosser Sache mich gemacht!
> Warum setzt' er Thuiskon mir in Brand?
> Ich will die höhnische Dämonenbrut nicht lieben!
> Solang' sie in Germanien trotzt,
> Ist Hass mein Amt und meine Tugend Rache! [clix].

He adopts every means at his disposal without a qualm and pursues
his aim vindictively and with barbaric cruelty. Part of his campaign
was based on the assumption that the Roman soldiers would act on
the same principles. He is taken aback when he learns that they
behave with discipline. He stirs up hatred among his own people
by disseminating false rumours about their misdeeds (Act II,
Scene 2) and when his provocations do not achieve the desired result
he exclaims:

> Verflucht sei diese Zucht mir der Kohorten!

Nothing could be more perverted than the use he makes of Hally's
dismembered body. He even employs his own wife as a political
cat's-paw (Act III, Scene 3), and after Thusnelda has taken her
gruesome revenge on Ventidius, a horrible deed of premeditated and
perverted hatred, not merely, as Penthesilea's slaughter of Achilles is,
a deed of perverted love, Hermann commends her heroism:

> Mein schönes Thuschen! Heldin grüss' ich dich!
> Wie gross und prächtig hast du Wort gehalten! [clx].

He is allowed to emerge from his enterprise physically and morally unscathed, except for a slight wound in his arm which he knows how to turn to account. In the sphere of national enterprise Kleist justifies that very practice of deceit which had filled him with misgivings in the period of his metaphysical pessimism.

Not many of the German critics who have examined this drama have commented on this stultification of Kleist's former values. They believe, with Kleist himself, that such values do not apply to life in the sphere of national endeavour. Meyer-Benfey justifies even the Hally incident and explains that Hermann had to sacrifice his own virtue and honesty in the interest of the national cause. 'Aber alle Falschheit ist nur Treue gegen das Vaterland.' [clxi]. This hypocrisy is a clear instance of what happens when the insistence on absolute and unconditional values, the 'Drang nach dem Absoluten', is relinquished or when this urge to attain the absolute is carried over into the world of political affairs. When patriotism becomes a mere substitute for metaphysics in the presentation of human life, we get that confusion of values and that disregard for true standards of ethical conduct which is so deplorable a feature of *Die Hermannsschlacht*.

But this work is not the only product of Kleist's patriotism. Patriotic feelings are a source of his inspiration in his last drama. They are, however, not its only, and perhaps they are not the most important source. *Prinz Friedrich von Homburg* is a noble and a serene product of Kleist's mature genius because propagandist motives were not the primary reasons for its composition.

VI

PRINZ FRIEDRICH VON HOMBURG

THE plot of *Prinz Friedrich von Homburg* is based on a passage contained in Frederick the Great's *Memoires pour servir à l'histoire de la Maison de Brandebourg*. It is worth while quoting this account of the battle of Fehrbellin, since the alterations which Kleist made when he dramatized it, are of great interest.

'Le 18. de Juin' writes Frederick about the Elector[1] 'il marche aux Suédois: il confie seize cens chevaux de son Avant garde au Prince de Hombourg, avec ordre de ne rien engager, mais de reconnoître l'Ennemi. Ce Prince part; et après avoir traversé un bois, il voit les troupes Suédoises campées entre les Villages de Hackenberg et de Tornow, aïant un marais à leur dos, le pont de Fehrbellin au-delà de leur droite, et une plaine rase devant leur front: il pousse les grandes gardes, les poursuit et les mene battant jusqu'au gros de leur Corps; les troupes sortent en même tems de leur Camp, et se rangent en bataille: le Prince de Hombourg, plein d'un courage brillant, s'abandonne à sa vivacité, et engage un combat qui auroit eu une fin funeste, si l'Electeur averti du danger dans lequel il se trouvoit, ne fut accouru à son secours.' The Elector at once made his dispositions, attacked with all his cavalry on the enemy's right. Frederick continues: 'Les Suédois se jetterent dans des marais où ils furent tués par les Païsans, et ceux qui se sauverent, s'enfuirent par Fehrbellin, où ils rompirent le pont derriere eux. — Il est digne de la majesté de l'Histoire, de rapporter la belle action que fit un Ecuïer de l'Electeur dans ce combat: l'Electeur montoit un cheval blanc: Froben son Ecuïer s'apperçut que les Suédois tiroient plus sur ce cheval, qui se distinguoit par sa couleur, que sur les autres: il pria son maître de le troquer contre le sien, sous prétexte que ce-lui de l'Electeur étoit ombrageux; et à peine ce fidele Domestique l'eut il monté quelques momens, qu'il fut tué et sauva ainsi par sa mort la vie à l'Electeur. — Ce Prince, qui n'avoit point d'Infanterie, ne put ni forcer le pont de Fehrbellin, ni poursuivre l'Ennemi dans sa fuite: il se contenta d'établir son camp sur ce champ de bataille, où il avoit acquis tant de gloire: il pardonna au Prince de Hombourg, d'avoir exposé avec tant de légereté la fortune de tout l'Etat, en lui disant: "Si je vous jugeois

---

[1] P. 147, *passim*, of the 1751 edition.

selon la rigueur des Loix militaires, vous auriez mérité de perdre la vie; mais à Dieu ne plaise que je ternisse l'éclat d'un jour aussi heureux, en répandant le sang d'un Prince qui a été un des principaux instrumens de ma victoire !" '

According to Frederick's account the Prince was in command of a small detachment of cavalry which was to act as a reconnoitring party. He attacks contrary to orders and the Elector intervenes when the battle is nearly won by the Swedes. In his drama Kleist completely changes the situation. Under Kottwitz Prince Friedrich commands the whole of the cavalry and it is he who intervenes, against the Elector's orders. He attacks at the moment when the enemy is in retreat and although he gains his own objective, he frustrates the plan by which the Elector had hoped to annihilate the Swedes. In Frederick the Great's account the Prince materially contributed to the victory, in *Prinz Friedrich von Homburg* he gains only a limited success and spoils the Elector's chances of a decisive triumph. Hence Kleist makes the Elector do what, according to Frederick the Great, he only might have done. The Prince is placed before a court martial, as a result of which he is condemned to death. Kleist was attracted to the story because it presented a case that was not a clear cut legal and moral issue, a case which, like that of *Michael Kohlhaas*, has two wrongs and two rights. When he wrote his drama he was primarily interested in motivating the Prince's transgression and in working out the effect of the court martial upon his character.

There are two reasons why Prince Friedrich attacks the Swedes at the wrong moment. His action is explained first by his character and secondly by the incident that had taken place on the night before the battle. These reasons are closely connected with one another, since the incident bears upon the development of the Prince's character. In the opening scenes of the play the two motives are stated and in the following Acts they are amplified, in the same way as the Leitmotive are treated in a musical composition.

Kleist's intention in presenting the Prince as a somnambulist has been much debated. It is held that this aspect of his personality detracts from his qualities as a hero. But Kleist purposely reveals his weaknesses at the beginning of the drama. It was his desire to show Friedrich first as an immature character, in order to portray his awakening to a sense of responsibility at a later stage. Two ambitions rule the Prince's life at the time when we first meet him, his aspirations as a soldier and his love for Natalie, but as his conduct in the first scenes of the play, particularly his attitude to Hohenzollern's remarks about the dream, indicates, his real life as yet takes place in the realm of his subconscious. He is not aware of the true nature of his own being. He cannot recall Natalie's name when he awakes from sleep-walking.

Hohenzollern Zum Henker, sprich! Lässt das Gesicht sich raten?
— Welch' eine Dame meinest du?
Der Prinz von Homburg   Gleichviel! Gleichviel!
Der Nam' ist mir, seit ich erwacht, entfallen [clxii].

When he mentions her later in the scene it is not in the same connection, and when he discovers that Natalie is the owner of the glove in his possession, he is genuinely surprised. He does not, as might be thought, hide her identity from Hohenzollern. He does not know it himself, although he had called her by name during his sleep-walking.

Kleist's use of somnambulism in the first scenes of *Prinz Friedrich von Homburg* differs considerably from his employment of the phenomenon in *Das Käthchen von Heilbronn*. In the scene under the elder tree the true facts concerning Wetter vom Strahl's and Käthchen's relationship are revealed. Through her trance the happy solution of all complications becomes possible. Here reality is revealed through the utterance of the somnambulist. In *Prinz Friedrich von Homburg* the tragic complications are caused by the somnambulist's experience. In the first scenes of the drama we have a glimpse of reality behind the somnambulist's interpretation of it and we see that this reality is a prank played by the Elector, a 'Scherz' which is as much a cause of Friedrich's future action as is his own character. We should go too far if we called this prank a piece of frivolous despotism, but it is an act of levity, and the Elector himself does not wish to have it spoken about. He sends his page to Hohenzollern with the request not to mention the affair to the Prince:

Dem Prinzen möchtet Ihr, wenn er erwacht,
Kein Wort, befiehlt er, von dem Scherz entdecken,
Den er sich eben jetzt mit ihm erlaubt! [clxiii].

The Elector cannot foresee the consequences of his behaviour, but as Hohenzollern is to point out to him later with dangerous frankness, it is the trick which he had played on Friedrich that is largely responsible for the Prince's absent-mindedness at the gathering of the commanders when the battle plan is explained to them and they receive their specific orders. At this gathering, by a strange circumstance, at two o'clock in the morning, the Elector's wife and Natalie are present and here Natalie misses her glove. Friedrich notices this when he should be listening to the Field Marshal's explanation of the task assigned to him. He cannot be exonerated from blame for paying attention to Natalie rather than to Dörfling; on the other hand he really does not know what had happened a few hours before. He mechanically repeats and writes down a few words of the command, but his mind is occupied with the incident and it has a powerful influence upon him. He believes that the dream was about to become reality and that Fortune had given him a token of her favour. His short monologue shows that the desires which had dwelt in his subconscious mind had become a deliberate purpose with him:

> Nun denn, auf deiner Kugel, Ungeheures,
> Du, der der Windeshauch den Schleier heut
> Gleich einem Segel, lüftet, roll' heran!
> Du hast mir, Glück, die Locken schon gestreift:
> Ein Pfand schon warfst du, im Vorüberschweben,
> Aus deinem Füllhorn lächelnd mir herab:
> Heut, Kind der Götter, such' ich, Flüchtiges,
> Ich hasche dich im Feld der Schlacht und stürze
> Ganz deinen Segen mir zu Füssen um:
> Wärst du auch siebenfach, mit Eisenketten,
> Am schwed'schen Siegeswagen festgebunden! [clxiv].

These circumstances explain his surprise when, at the beginning of the battle, he realizes that the rôle which he has been assigned is a passive one hindering the achievement of his ambition. Again he falls into a reverie when Hohenzollern explains the battle order to him:

> *Der Prinz von Homburg* Was ich dir sagen wollte, Heinrich —
> 　　　　　(Er führt den Grafen ein wenig vor)
> 　　Was war's schon, was der Dörfling, mich betreffend,
> 　　Bei der Parol' hat gestern vorgebracht?
> *Hohenzollern* Du warst zerstreut. Ich hab' es wohl gesehn.
> *Der Prinz von Homburg* Zerstreut — geteilt; ich weiss nicht, was mir
> 　　fehlte.
> 　　Diktieren in die Feder macht mich irr. —

Hohenzollern Zum Glück nicht diesmal eben viel für dich.
   Der Truchss und Hennings, die das Fussvolk führen,
   Die sind zum Angriff auf den Feind bestimmt,
   Und dir ist aufgegeben, hier zu halten
   Im Tal, schlagfertig mit der Reuterei,
   Bis man zum Angriff den Befehl dir schickt.
Der Prinz von Homburg (nach einer Pause, in der er vor sich niederge-
  —Ein wunderlicher Vorfall!¹ [clxv].   [träumt)

He is again preoccupied with the incident and with the part he
desires to play, the part, he believes, assigned to him by Fortune.
When the battle goes well for the Prussians, the passivity to which
he is condemned irks him more and more and when Wrangel begins
to retreat, the Prince, fearing that the victory would be won without
him, disregarding the greater issues at stake, forces Kottwitz, his
commander, to give the signal for the cavalry attack. After an initial
setback a brilliant victory is won, but, as the Elector points out later,
this attack frustrated his plan to annihilate the Swedes completely:

   Den Obrist Hennings hatt' ich abgeschickt,
   Wie dir bekannt, den schwed'schen Brückenkopf,
   Der Wrangels Rücken deckt, hinwegzunehmen.
   Wenn ihr die Ordre nicht gebrochen hättet,
   Dem Hennings wäre dieser Schlag geglückt;
   Die Brücken hätt', er, in zwei Stunden Frist,
   In Brand gesteckt, am Rhyn sich aufgepflanzt,
   Und Wrangel wäre ganz mit Stumpf und Stiel
   In Gräben und Morast, vernichtet worden. [clxvi].

Kottwitz is unable to answer this charge except with a lame excuse:

   Es ist der Stümper Sache, nicht die deine,
   Des Schicksals höchsten Kranz erringen wollen [clxvii].

¹ A close examination of the play reveals several curious inconsistencies. In Acts I and II
the Prince's position as leader of the cavalry, and the timing of the events before the battle are
differently represented in different places. In addition, there is the episode of Homburg's fall
from his horse, an accident which has no influence on the action except that it gives rise to
the rumour about the Prince's absence from the battle-field and this accounts for the Elector's
surprise at seeing him after the engagement. Similarly, it is strange that the Prince should excuse
his lack of attention at the generals' meeting with the words: 'Diktieren in die Feder macht mich
irr.' This is obviously not the real reason for his absent-mindedness. Hohenzollern does not,
as we should expect, reply that he had witnessed the whole incident and knew the true explanation. Niejahr undoubtedly goes too far in assuming that Hohenzollern was not in the play at an
earlier stage of its conception and that Scenes 1–4 of Act I and Scene 5 of Act V were added
to a hypothetical earlier version. But he has good reason for believing that Kleist had a different
conception of the Elector's share in Homburg's guilt when he began to write the play and that
he emphasized this aspect at a later stage in the composition. If this assumption is correct,
then we have a repetition of the process clearly manifested in the composition of *Penthesilea*,
namely the insertion of a new argument motivating the hero's guilt, the addition of an external
cause to the purely inward action previously presented in the drama.

and with the prediction that on the next occasion Wrangel would be totally defeated. For, he smugly adds

> Rom ward an einem Tage nicht erbaut. [clxviii].

Prince Friedrich is therefore guilty not only of insubordination (a breach he will not tolerate in others when *he* gives a command, as his behaviour towards the First Officer before the attack shows) but also of having delayed the final defeat of Wrangel's army. His action on the battlefield was dictated by selfish motives. His argument, compelling Kottwitz to comply with his desire to attack, should be noted:

> Auf Ordr'! Ei, Kottwitz! Reitest du so langsam?
> Hast du sie noch vom Herzen nicht empfangen? [clxix].

The point that orders can be disobeyed when the heart dictates another course is a principle of anarchy and insubordination. It is, perhaps, not surprising that the immature and impulsive Prince should hold such a view, but it is strange that a seasoned soldier like Kottwitz should agree with him. For in his interview with the Elector in the fifth scene of the last Act Kottwitz defends the Prince's action on precisely the same grounds:

> Die schlechte,
> Kurzsicht'ge Staatskunst, die, um eines Falles,
> Da die Empfindung sich verderblich zeigt,
> Zehn andere vergisst, im Lauf der Dinge,
> Da die Empfindung einzig retten kann! [clxx].

It is often said that one of Kleist's purposes in writing *Prinz Friedrich von Homburg* was to demonstrate the validity of this point of view, to defend the claims of feeling against those of reason and to protest against the rigid enforcement of disciplinary rules. This view is probably correct, but it is not the whole truth. There is another side to the question, and indeed the outstanding quality of this play in the body of Kleist's dramatic work consists in the fact that nowhere else are right and wrong so evenly distributed among the principal characters, as here. Kottwitz' opinion, which is later reiterated by Natalie, that feelings should be allowed full sway, is entirely subjective. In the circumstances in which Kottwitz advances his views, he defends a principle of anarchy. This is made quite clear by the Elector in his conversation with Kottwitz:

Meinst du, das Glück werd' immerdar, wie jüngst,
Mit einem Kranz den Ungehorsam lohnen?
Den Sieg nicht mag ich, der, ein Kind des Zufalls,
Mir von der Bank fällt: das Gesetz will ich,
Die Mutter meiner Krone, aufrecht halten,
Die ein Geschlecht von Siegen mir erzeugt! [clxxi].

Kottwitz is by no means the ideal soldier that he is sometimes made out to be. He is a cantankerous old gentleman who rebukes his superiors when he thinks fit:

Golz Hast du den Marschall Dörfling aufgefunden?
Obrist Kottwitz (kommt vorwärts): Zum Henker, nein! Was denkt die
    Exzellenz?
Bin ich ein Pfeil, ein Vogel, ein Gedanke,
Dass er mich durch das ganze Schlachtfeld sprengt? [clxxii].

and he gives a wrong analysis of the situation existing before he commanded the cavalry to attack:

Die Schweden wankten, auf dem linken Flügel,
Und auf dem rechten wirkten sie Sukkurs;
Hätt'er auf deine Ordre warten wollen,
Sie fassten Posten wieder, in den Schluchten,
Und nimmermehr hätt'st du den Sieg erkämpft. [clxiii].

The Elector has the full measure of his man and treats him with kindness. 'Mit dir' he says 'du alter wunderlicher Herr, Werd' ich nicht fertig!' [clxiv]. He prefers in the end to convince Kottwitz through the mouth of the Prince himself.

The Elector rightly cannot accept Kottwitz' plea. Ultimately it is Hohenzollern to whose argument he must listen. Hohenzollern bases his defence not on a principle, but on the particular circumstances which influenced the Prince and for which the Elector himself was largely responsible. As he was not aware of Friedrich's secret desires, he could not foresee the results of his own indiscretion, but he cannot be exonerated from blame, and he is not insensible of his responsibility. When Hohenzollern describes the scene at headquarters and informs him that the glove belonged to Natalie, 'der Kurfürst fällt in Gedanken' [clxxv] and after Dörfling has substantiated the story, he vents his exasperation for the first and only time:

Tor, der du bist, Blödsinniger! Hättest du
Nicht in den Garten mich herabgerufen,
So hätt' ich, einem Trieb der Neugier folgend,

> Mit diesem Träumer harmlos nicht gescherzt.
> Mithin behaupt' ich ganz mit gleichem Recht,
> Der sein Versehn veranlasst hat, warest du! —
> Die delph'sche Weisheit meiner Offiziere! [clxxvi].

What he had called the Prince's 'Frevel' he now terms a 'Versehen'
and he does not reply to Hohenzollern's remark:

> Es ist genug, mein Kurfürst! Ich bin sicher,
> Mein Wort fiel, ein Gewicht, in deine Brust! [clxxvii].

Before Kottwitz and Hohenzollern put forward their different
pleas in favour of the Prince, a development has taken place of which
they are ignorant but which is known to the Elector. This is a change
in Homburg's attitude to his behaviour on the battlefield and to its
consequences. As long as he is flushed with exultation over his share
in the victory, the wrongness of his disobedience does not strike him.
Success is his justification. He is therefore completely taken aback
when he is taken under arrest and deprived of military honours. At
first he tries to explain his imprisonment as a piece of formality with
which the Elector had to comply and, as before, he puts his trust in
the superior claims of feeling, believing that the Elector will put
feelings before duty:

> Der Kurfürst hat getan, was Pflicht erheischte,
> Und nun wird er dem Herzen auch gehorchen. [clxxviii].

and

> Das Kriegsrecht musste auf den Tod erkennen;
> So lautet das Gesetz, nach dem es richtet.
> Doch eh' er solch ein Urteil lässt vollstrecken,
> Eh' er dies Herz hier, das getreu ihn liebt,
> Auf eines Tuches Wink, der Kugel preisgibt,
> Eh', sieh, eh' öffnet er die eigne Brust sich
> Und sprützt sein eigen Blut selbst tropfenweis in Staub. [clxxix]

When Hohenzollern assures him that the Elector is on the point of
signing the death sentence and that there is no likelihood of a
reprieve, the Prince's sanguine trust in the validity of his feelings gives
way to despair. He believes that his love for Natalie is the cause of
his downfall, and not his act of insubordination, and he suspects
the Elector of vindictiveness on this account. He debases himself
before the Kurfürstin, renounces Natalie, and suffers a complete
moral collapse when he sees the open grave. He sends Natalie to
the Elector to plead for him, resigns his position in the army and

his claims on Natalie's love—the two objects of his former aspiration. He clings to the barest desire to live.

Natalie makes the same plea for Friedrich as Kottwitz and the Prince himself:

> Das Kriegsgesetz, das weiss ich wohl, soll herrschen,
> Jedoch die lieblichen Gefühle auch. [clxxx].

As formulated by her, this principle has greater validity than it has when Kottwitz enunciates it. Although she comes dangerously near to raising the standard of rebellion, she is a balanced personality, one of the most convincing female characters portrayed by Kleist.

When the Elector learns from her that Homburg has yielded to despair, he is utterly surprised and confused. As some critics have pointed out, his consternation is caused by his scruples about the justness of the death sentence; but to an even greater extent it is an effect of his realization that he had misjudged the Prince's character. He realizes that the execution of a soldier in Homburg's state of mind would not achieve the aim he had in mind, to enforce discipline in the army. However, he quickly recovers from his confusion and not without a touch of irony agrees to pardon the Prince if he really considers the sentence unjust:

> Bei meinem Eid! Ich schwör's dir zu! Wo werd' ich
> Mich gegen solchen Kriegers Meinung setzen?
> Die höchste Achtung, wie dir wohl bekannt,
> Trag' ich im Innersten für sein Gefühl.
> Wenn er den Spruch für ungerecht kann halten,
> Kassier' ich die Artikel: er ist frei! — [clxxxi].

He requests the Prince to say that the verdict was wrong, not that he, Friedrich, was innocent. In his letter to Friedrich he subtly appeals to the Prince's sense of responsibility and honour:

> 'Mein Prinz von Homburg, als ich Euch gefangen setzte
> Um Eures Angriffs, allzufrüh vollbracht,
> Da glaubt' ich nichts, als meine Pflicht zu tun;
> Auf Euren eignen Beifall rechnet' ich.
> Meint Ihr, ein Unrecht sei Euch widerfahren,
> So bitt' ich, sagt's mir mit zwei Worten —
> Und gleich den Degen schick' ich Euch zurück.' [clxxxii].

and Homburg, confronted with a situation in which his personal integrity is tested for the first time, refuses to make such a statement:

>Dass er mir unrecht tat, wie's mir bedingt wird,
>Das kann ich ihm nicht schreiben. [clxxxiii].

He now recognizes both his guilt and the ambiguity of his present situation:

>Schuld ruht, bedeutende, mir auf der Brust,
>Wie ich es wohl erkenne; kann er mir
>Vergeben nur, wenn ich mit ihm drum streite,
>So mag ich nichts von seiner Gnade wissen. [clxxxiv].

Natalie's hastiness, her urgency in desiring him to write the letter, only confirm him in his newly-won assurance.

This development in the Prince's character is clearly indicated without undue elaboration by means of monologues or asides. The tense and suggestive atmosphere in the prison chamber alone suffices to portray Friedrich's moral rehabilitation and the growth of his sense of duty. Together with the Kurfürst's recognition of his own responsibility, Homburg's atonement forms the basis of the dramatic dénouement. In the last scenes of Act V the first scenes of Act I repeat themselves, but what had been a somnambulist's dream becomes a soldier's reality. Restored to his command and assured of possessing Natalie, Prince Friedrich is acclaimed the victor of Fehrbellin. His ambitions have been realized because he is a different man. A selfish dream has become a just reward.

In *Prinz Friedrich von Homburg* Kleist presents a moral solution of a legal problem. Strictly speaking he has shelved the problem itself. Homburg's voluntary submission to the law is not a good reason for his pardon, and much less a reason for rewarding him with those things for which he had broken the law. But the situation is complicated by virtue of the Elector's own position. As an absolute ruler, the commander-in-chief of the army, he can punish or pardon, as he thinks fit. When Natalie appeals to his tender feelings and he replies

>Dich aber frag' ich selbst: darf ich den Spruch,
>Den das Gericht gefällt, wohl unterdrücken? [clxxxv].

he is thinking of the political, not the legal side of the question. Whatever the guilt itself may be, he can act upon a legal verdict or not, as he desires. Expediency is his guiding principle and *qua* Elector he is a power above and beyond the law. Homburg, not without justification, likens him to a god:

>Wie könnt' er doch vor diesen Tisch mich laden,
>Von Richtern, herzlos, die, den Eulen gleich,

Stets von der Kugel mir das Grablied singen:
Dächt' er, mit einem heitern Herrscherspruch,
Nicht, als ein Gott, in ihren Kreis zu treten? [clxxxvi]

The Elector is by no means a tyrant, however, not 'der Dey von
Tunis,' but a humane and enlightened ruler. Nevertheless he is almost
cruel in his treatment of Natalie and Homburg even after he has torn
up the death sentence. He deliberately permits the enactment of all
the preparations for the execution. The death march is played and
the Prince's eyes are bandaged and only at the last moment is he
allowed to know that he has been reprieved. Naturally enough, he
faints. The Elector has permitted himself another 'Scherz' and in
the circumstances it is a crueller prank than his first caprice. Kleist
makes him behave as he had made Wetter vom Strahl behave towards
Käthchen when he deliberately misleads her into believing that he
would marry some one else and only tells her the truth at the wedding
ceremony. This delight in torture is an attribute of those characters
in Kleist's dramas, who have power and authority, and his use of it in
Das Käthchen von Heilbronn and *Prinz Friedrich von Homburg* is not
insignificant. These two dramas represent the dissolution of his tragic
perceptions, particularly of his misgivings about the intervention
of a malicious deity in the affairs of men. Wetter vom Strahl's and
the Elector's cruelty recalls to mind Kleist's tragic theme of divine
victimization, but it is now of minor importance.

Prinz Friedrich von Homburg, a work so different in theme and
treatment, in the atmosphere and style of life, from any of Kleist's
previous dramas, is a more authentic document of the progress of his
mind and art than *Das Käthchen von Heilbronn*. It represents the final
dissolution of his disharmonies. A drama without metaphysical
import and therefore free from those metaphysical questionings
which were the source of his tragedies, and no less of *Käthchen von
Heilbronn*, it demonstrates his newly-won belief in the values of self-
knowledge and self-subordination, and in the possibility of correcting
error. When error was no longer viewed by him as the lot of
humanity, but recognized as an attribute of human behaviour in
individual cases under certain circumstances, then he triumphed over
that sense of the tragic in life which Kant's philosophy had inspired
in him. He had won through to the knowledge that error can be
the stepping-stone to a higher achievement.

This positive belief on Kleist's part in the efficacy of human
endeavour is often taken to mean that he was in agreement with
Kant's categorical imperative, and that his solution of the conflict

H

between desire and duty is even more optimistic than Schiller's
answer to the same problem, since for him the conquest of desire
made true living possible, whereas for Schiller such a triumph could
be achieved only through death. Homburg's statement is truly in the
spirit of Kant's ethics:

> Ich will das heilige Gesetz des Kriegs,
> Das ich verletzt' im Angesicht des Heers,
> Durch einen freien Tod verherrlichen! [clxxxvii].

and his attitude to the Elector as expressed in his words:

> Er handle, wie er darf;
> Mir ziemt's hier zu verfahren, wie ich soll! [clxxxviii].

reminds us of a passage in Schiller's *Über Anmut und Würde*:

> Die blosse Macht, sei sie auch noch so furchtbar und grenzenlos, kann
> nie Majestät verleihen. Macht imponiert nur dem Sinnenwesen, die
> Majestät muss dem Geist seine Freiheit nehmen. Ein Mensch, der mir das
> Todesurteil schreiben kann, hat darum noch keine Majestät für mich,
> sobald ich selbst nur bin, was ich sein soll. Sein Vorteil über mich ist aus,
> sobald ich will. Wer mir aber in seiner Person den reinen Willen darstellt,
> vor dem werde ich mich, wenn's möglich ist, auch noch in künftigen
> Welten beugen.[1] [clxxxix].

Majesty is for Schiller 'der höchste Grad der Würde' which is a
manifestation of the sublime. If Kleist is in agreement with Schiller
on the qualities of majesty and expresses his view in the figure of the
Elector, then, we may say, he has, in *Prinz Friedrich von Homburg*
adopted the Kantian conception of sublimity in the place of Burke's
or Adam Müller's view, which he had hitherto held. But he has
gone further. Just as he had changed Schiller's principle of 'Anmut'
into his own idea of 'Grazie' in *Über das Marionettentheater*, so he has
produced a new fusion of will and obedience, desire and duty, feeling
and reason in his last drama. For the first time in his work the
principal actors are a protagonist and an antagonist in the true sense
of these terms, not merely partners in an incomprehensible mas-
querade. Their conflicts are real and practical, not a combat with
frightening shadows, and the solution of these conflicts is a result of
their mutual accommodation based on the recognition of their own
failings.

In a drama revealing so much objectivity and substance, Kleist
achieved a new perfection of form and style. Without losing his
power of expressiveness he was able to evoke a feeling of detachment

---

[1] *Werke, Säkularausgabe*, Vol. XI, pp. 242 f.

and serenity. When we compare this play with Kleist's previous dramas, we are struck by the evenness of its tone. There are many surprising episodes such as Friedrich's reaction to the death-sentence and to the Elector's letter, and Natalie's initiative in assembling the members of her regiment, but none has the shrillness, the pathological quality that characterizes the incidents in Kleist's earlier work. This fundamental sanity is not jeopardized by the much debated attitude of the Prince to death, nor by his somnambulism, and it strongly colours the love scenes in this play which are not less poetical for being genuinely natural. The language employed in this drama, too, possesses a wider range than that of Kleist's other work; his medium has become supple and varied and it admirably expresses the sentiments characteristic of members of the army, the court and of polite society. It expresses official as well as private relationship with ease and vigour. Kleist's images have lost none of their former power and succinctness, and they have gained in poetic quality. This may be seen when we compare the imagery employed in *Penthesilea* with that contained in *Prinz Friedrich von Homburg*. It is less forceful, but it is also less strident in Kleist's last work.

He called the play a 'Schauspiel'. This drama therefore takes its place, and it takes its place worthily, beside Lessing's 'dramatic poem' *Nathan der Weise* and Goethe's 'Schauspiele' *Iphigenie auf Tauris* and *Torquato Tasso*. The dramatic developments in all these plays have high seriousness and they constantly verge upon tragedy. But unmistakably, from the outset, they also tend towards a solution of the tragic problem lying at the core of the action. Kleist's solution in *Prinz Friedrich von Homburg* is not without moral ambiguity, but aesthetically it is thoroughly convincing. This is most clearly felt in the parallel scenes opening and closing the work—so similar and yet so markedly different in content and tone. The one inevitably leads into tragic complications, the other no less naturally emerges from them into reconciliation.

EPILOGUE

IN the light of the final development of his work, indicating a greater measure of affirmation than any of his previous efforts, it is customary to seek an explanation for Kleist's suicide in a renewal of his pessimism. Indeed, the failure of the *Berliner Abendblätter*, upon the success of which he had staked so much, his disappointment when his offers to serve as a lieutenant in the Prussian army were disregarded, his disillusionment when the King of Prussia decided to support Napoleon in his campaign against Russia, instead of waging war against France, all these factors played their part in Kleist's determination to end his life. But while, in the last resort, his suicide must remain a mystery, the letters which he wrote before he took his own life and that of Adolfine Henriette Vogel, as well as the report of the innkeeper at Stimmings, support the view that Kleist committed suicide not only in a moment of depression, because he saw no prospect in life, but also in a state of ecstasy and elation.

Throughout his life he had suffered from an inability to establish permanent contacts with men and women. When we examine his letters to Wilhelmine von Zenge, Ulrike, Heinrich Lohse, Marie von Kleist and others, we find that he always demanded more from his friends than they were prepared to give. The weaker side of his character is revealed in his tendency to assess the value of his relationships according to the readiness of his friends to make a sacrifice. In a letter to Wilhelmine von Zenge, dated January 31, 1801, he painted a characteristic picture of the devotion of his friend Brockes and he ends with the enumeration of the following 'glorious principles': 'Wahre Uneigennützigkeit zeigt sich in dem Talent, sich durch den Eigennutz Andrer nie gekränkt zu fühlen, eben so gut, ja selbst noch besser, als in dem Talent ihm immer zuvor zu kommen. Daher klage den Andern nie um dieser Untugend an. Wenn er Dein freiwilliges Opfer nicht versteht, so schweige und zürne nicht, und wenn er ein Opfer von Dir verlangt, vorausgesetzt dass es nur möglich ist, so tue es, und er mag es Dir danken, oder nicht, schweige wieder und zürne nicht.' [cxc]. Käthchen is indeed the imaginative realization of Kleist's ideal of womanhood.

In his farewell letters to Marie von Kleist (November 9th, 10th, and 12th, 1811) he says of his sister Ulrike: 'Sie hat, dünkt mich, die Kunst nicht verstanden sich aufzuopfern, ganz für das, was man

liebt, in Grund und Boden zu gehn: das Seligste, was sich auf Erden
erdenken lässt, ja worin der Himmel bestehen muss, wenn es wahr ist,
dass man darin vergnügt und glücklich ist.' [cxci]. In Henriette
Vogel he found a woman, for the first time in his life, who was
prepared to make the sacrifice he demanded. When we remember
that she was by no means an attractive woman, the apostrophe which
he wrote to her in Berlin ('nach Michaelis 1810') might be considered the most unintelligible piece of extravagant adulation, were it
not for the fact that her readiness to die with him made her 'mein
Alles und Jedes, mein Weib, meine Hochzeit, die Taufe meiner
Kinder, mein Trauerspiel, mein Nachruhm.' [cxcii]. To Marie von
Kleist he wrote:

> Rechne hinzu, dass ich eine Freundin gefunden habe, deren Seele wie
> ein junger Adler fliegt, wie ich noch in meinen Leben nichts ähnliches
> gefunden habe; die meine Traurigkeit als eine höhere, festgewurzelte und
> unheilbare begreift, und deshalb, obschon sie Mittel genug in Händen hätte
> mich hier zu beglücken, mit mir sterben will, die mir die unerhörte Lust
> gewährt, sich, um dieses Zweckes Willen, so leicht aus einer ganz wunsch-
> losen Lage, wie ein Veilchen aus einer Wiese, heraus heben zu lassen . . .
> und Du wirst begreifen, dass meine ganze jauchzende Sorge nur sein kann,
> einen Abgrund tief genug zu finden, um mit ihr hinab zu stürzen.
>
> Ach, ich versichere Dich, ich bin ganz selig. Morgens und Abends knie
> ich nieder, was ich nie gekonnt habe, und bete zu Gott; ich kann ihm mein
> Leben, das allerqualvollste, das je ein Mensch geführt hat, jetzo danken,
> weil er es mir durch den herrlichsten und wollüstigsten aller Tode vergü-
> tigt . . . Der Entschluss, der in ihrer Seele aufging, mit mir zu sterben, zog
> mich, ich kann Dir nicht sagen, mit welcher unaussprechlichen und un-
> widerstehlichen Gewalt, an ihre Brust, erinnerst Du Dich wohl, dass ich
> Dich mehrmals gefragt habe, ob Du mit mir sterben willst? — Aber Du
> sagtest immer nein — [cxciii].

As a poet Kleist achieved the pinnacle of his self-realization in the
composition of *Prinz Friedrich von Homburg*. His death may elicit our
sympathy, but it yet exposes the essential weakness and the egoism
of the man. Traces of these qualities are not absent from his poetic
work. They often disturb and repel us in the midst of much that is
genuinely great, elevated and pure. *Prinz Friedrich von Homburg* is
Kleist's masterpiece because it is almost entirely free from the contamination of his psychological infirmities, because its poetic sources
are the nobler mainsprings of his arresting personality, revealing his
self-mastery in the presentation of life.

TRANSLATION OF PASSAGES QUOTED

[i] *Essay on finding the safe road to happiness*: Somewhere in the Universe there must be a basis for happiness, the sum total of things, my friend, must contain within itself the causes and the elements of happiness, for the Deity will not disappoint the yearning for this happiness which it has itself inextinguishably kindled in our souls. Vol. IV, p. 58.

[ii] I hear a thousand people talking and I see how they act and it does not occur to me to ask for the reason. They do not know it themselves. Obscure inclinations guide them and the moment determines their actions. They remain for ever in a state of minority and their fate a plaything of chance. They feel that they are guided and drawn along by invisible powers. In their feeling of impotence they follow these powers wherever they may lead them, to a happiness which they only half enjoy, to misfortune which becomes doubly painful to them. This servile submission to the whims of the tyrant Fate is indeed entirely unworthy of a free and thinking human being. A free and thinking human being does not stay where chance has pushed him, or else, if he does stay there, he stays for good reasons, because it is the better choice. He feels that one can rise superior to Fate and even that it is possible in the truest sense of the word to guide one's Fate.—Indeed, I cannot understand at all how a human being can live without having a plan of life. The feeling of certainty with which I utilize the present moment, the tranquillity with which I face the future, make me realize so warmly the inestimable happiness that my plan of life bestows upon me; a situation without a plan of life, without a fixed destiny, always to oscillate between unstable desires, always to be at variance with my duties, a plaything of chance, a puppet on the string of Fate—this ignoble situation seems to me to be so contemptible, and would make me so unhappy that death would appear to me much more preferable. Vol. V, pp. 41, 43 f.

[iii] You hear me talk at length and enthusiastically about virtue and yet I know that you only attach an obscure meaning to this word. Dear friend, although I talk so much about it, I do not fare any better than you. To me it only appears to be something great, sublime, ineffable, something for which I vainly seek a word in order to express it by means of language, vainly seek a shape in order to express it by means of an image. And yet I strive towards it with the innermost warmth of my being, as if it stood clearly and distinctly before my soul. All I know about it is that it will certainly contain the imperfect ideas which I am now capable of conceiving. But I have a presentiment of something more, something higher, more sublime, and it is really and truly this that I cannot express and shape. . . . And now, my friend, let me put a proposition to you, of

the truth of which my mind is convinced, although my heart continually contradicts it. This is the proposition that of all the paths lying between the highest material happiness and misfortune we should wander along the middle path alone and should never direct our desires towards the giddy heights. However much I now hate middle paths of all kinds because a naturally vehement urge within me beguiles me, I yet have a feeling that time and experience will one day convince me that these middle paths are the best. Vol. IV, pp. 60, 65.

[iv] Now, indeed, we stagger about on our irregular courses, but, my friend, since we are young, we cannot be blamed. The inward fermentation of interacting forces which fills us at our age, admits of no peace in thought and deed. We do not yet know the magic formula and time alone will produce it for us, by which we may pacify and calm the strangely heterogeneous shapes stirring and whirling within us. And all young men whom we see beside and around us share this fate with us. All their paces and movements appear to be no more than the effects of an impalpable but violent thrust that irresistibly carries them along. They appear to me to be like comets which spin through the universe in irregular rotations until at last they find a settled course and a law of motion. Vol. IV, p. 66.

[v] It is unprofitable and often calamitous even for men to reflect upon the purpose of the whole of our eternal existence, to inquire whether, as Epicure thought, the enjoyment of happiness, or, as Leibniz believed, the achievement of perfection, or, as Kant asserts, the performance of mere duty is the final goal of man . . . Consider for yourself, how can we, who are but finite beings and can survey only an infinitely small portion of eternity, our existence on earth, how can we venture to fathom the plan which nature designed for eternity? And if that is impossible, how can a just Deity demand from us that we intervene in this eternal plan, demand this from us who are not even able to form an idea of it? But we can without question find out what is the purpose of our earthly existence and the Deity can therefore justly demand that we should fulfil this purpose. Vol. V, p. 127.

[vi] That a God exists, that there are such things as an eternal life, a reward for virtue, a punishment for vice, all these are propositions . . . which we can therefore do without. For surely we should do without them, according to the will of the Deity itself, since the Deity itself has made it impossible for us to understand and to comprehend all. Would you no longer do what is right if the notions of God and eternity prove to be mere dreams? I should not. Vol V, p. 130.

[vii] We cannot decide whether what we call truth is truly true or whether it only appears so to us. If the latter is the case, then the truth which we gather here on earth no longer exists in death—and all our efforts to acquire a possession which will follow us into the grave are vain. Alas, Wilhelmine, if the edge of this thought does not strike your heart, do not smile about another, whom it has wounded in the depths of his sacred

being. My sole, my highest aim has vanished and now I possess none. Vol. V, p. 204.

[viii] Life is the only possession which is worth something only if we do not respect it, Whoever loves it with care is already morally dead, for his supreme power of life, namely the power to sacrifice life, disintegrates while he tends it. And yet—alas, how incomprehensible is the will that rules over us!—This enigmatic something that we possess, we do not know from whom, that leads us on, we do not know whither, that is our property, we do not know whether we can dispose of it, a chattel which is of no value if we value it, an object that is like a paradox, shallow and profound, barren and fertile, worthy and contemptible, ambiguous and inexhaustible, an object which everybody would like to cast away like an unintelligible book, are we not bound by a law of nature to love it? Vol. V, p. 244.

[ix] In truth, when we consider that we require a whole lifetime in order to learn how to live, that even in death we have no notion of heaven's intentions with us, when nobody knows the goal of his life or his destiny, when human reason does not suffice to comprehend itself, the soul, life, and the things around it, when after millenia we still question the existence of right—can God demand responsibility from such creatures? . . . What can it really mean to do evil, as far as the effects are concerned? What is evil? Absolute evil? Vol. V, p. 249.

[x] The relativization of the concept of truth is obviously the exact opposite of the aim of critical philosophy, both historically and systematically.

[xi] Enjoyment! This is the prize of life! Indeed, if we never rejoice in life, may we not justifiably ask the Creator: why didst Thou give it to me? It is the duty of God to grant His creatures enjoyment of life, the duty of man to deserve it. Indeed, an obligation is laid upon man to do something good: understand me well, I am not speaking figuratively, simply to do something. I shall understand that more and more clearly, learn to feel it more and more vividly, until my reason and my heart with the whole power of my soul effect a resolve in me. Vol. V, p. 250.

[xii] When we gaze, with eyes refreshed and restored by the Greeks, upon the highest spheres of the world swirling around us, we observe how the lust for insatiable optimistic cognition which is revealed in Socrates in such an exemplary manner, suddenly changes into tragic resignation and a desire for artistic expression. . . . The immense courage and wisdom of Kant and Schopenhauer succeeded in gaining the most arduous victory, the victory over the optimism concealed in the nature of logic. This optimism again is the basis of our civilization. While in the optimistic view which was based on the aeternae veritates that were unquestioningly accepted, it was thought that all the riddles of the world could be understood and explained, . . . Kant revealed how these eternal truths really only served to raise mere semblance, the work of Maja, into the position of sole and supreme reality, and to put it in the place of the innermost and

real essence of all things . . . With this recognition a civilization has been inaugurated which I venture to call tragic. Its most characteristic feature is to substitute, as the highest aim, in the place of science, that wisdom which is not deluded by the enticing distractions of science, and with immovable gaze turns to the total aspect of the world, and with sympathetic love seeks to comprehend the eternal suffering therein as its own suffering . . . That with the phrases of Kant and Schopenhauer I laboriously sought to express new and alien valuations which were incompatible with the spirit of Kant and Schopenhauer, as well as with their taste.

[xiii]   For a few weeks it has seemed to me that the storm has somewhat abated. Vol. V, p. 246.

[xiv]   Meanwhile I feel more and more serene from day to day and I hope that nature will at last grant me that measure of happiness which she owes to all her creatures. Vol. V, p. 258.

[xv]   I have suddenly interrupted the course of my studies and shall make up for lost time here, not merely for the sake of truth, but for a more humane purpose. Vol. V, p. 250.

[xvi]   A great desire has stirred in me, without the gratification of which I shall never be happy. This is to do something good. Indeed, I firmly believe that this desire has hitherto always been the obscure basis of my sorrow and that I have only now become really aware of it. An obligation rests upon human beings, which, like a debt of honour, continually exhorts every one who possesses a sense of honour. Vol. V, p. 259.

[xvii]   Tell me what you think, Wilhelmine; I still possess some of my capital, only a little, it is true, but it will suffice to buy a farm, perhaps in Switzerland, which will sustain me if I work it myself. Vol. V, p. 262.

[xviii]   It looked very much as though Switzerland, together with the Cisalpine territories, would become French and the very idea sickens me. Vol. V, p. 282.

[xix]   This is what I meant to tell you: I am actually so enamoured of the idea of tilling a field that it must be realized. Look upon my heart as an invalid and upon this desire as a little piece of cupidity which one can surely allow, if it is harmless . . . Seriously, when I consider my last year, when I consider how strangely embittered I have been about myself and about everything that surrounded me, I am tempted to believe that I really am ill. Vol. V, p. 275 f.

[xx]   I shall probably never return to my native country. As a rule you women do not understand one word in the German language, and that is ambition. In one case only I shall return and that is if I can satisfy the expectations which I have foolishly aroused in people by a number of boastful enterprises. It is a possible, but not a probable case. In short, if I cannot turn up in my country covered with glory, I shall never do so. That has been decided like the nature of my soul. Vol. V, p. 288 f.

[xxi]   (1) One spectacle particularly impresses me. The river Main

runs a straight course from the bridge and as swift as an arrow, as if it had its goal in view, as if nothing could stop it from reaching its goal, as if it desired to reach it impatiently by the shortest route—but a vine-clad hill deflects its impetuous course gently, yet with firm mind, as a wife arrests the impetuous will of her husband, and with noble constancy shows the way which will lead to the ocean—and the river obeys these modest injunctions, follows the kindly directions and abandons its premature goal and does not break through the hill, but circumvents it and, flowing more calmly, kisses its flowery feet.

(2) Dresden occupies a splendid and solemn position in the midst of a garland of hills which surround the town at some distance, as if they respectfully refrained from approaching too near. The river Elbe suddenly abandons its right bank and rapidly turns to Dresden, to embrace its darling. From the heights of the Zwinger one can follow the river's course nearly as far as Meissen. It turns now to the right, now to the left bank, as if it had to make a difficult choice and it staggers as if in ecstasy and playfully meanders, winding a thousand times through the pleasant valley, as if it did not wish to reach the ocean. . . . Like a virgin appearing among men, so the bright and slender Elbe appears among the rocks. Gently and with modest hesitation she approaches, the coarse race of men push forward and around her to bar the way and to peer into her pure and shining face. But she, without tarrying, slips through them fleetingly, blushing.

(3) And tearing itself away from the deep abysses of Plauen, like a secret desire from the bosom's depths, and hurled against rocks as if against prejudices, murmuring not in anger but with some annoyance, the Weiss-ritz winds indefatigably through all the obstacles until it emerges into the freedom of daylight, spreads out in the open country and, fulfilling its destiny, flows freely and quietly into the ocean. . . . Quiet, broad and majestic the Rhine approaches at Bingen and, confident like a hero of his victory and slowly, as if assured that it would complete its course—but a mountain range (the Hundsrück) throws itself into its path like calumny into the path of irreproachable virtue, and the rocks make way before it and look down upon it with surprise and admiration—but the river hurries past them contemptuously yet without exulting, and the only revenge in which it indulges is to show them their black image in its clear mirror. Vol. V, pp. 145, 223 f., 236 f.

[xxii] It must avoid the sandbanks of Inconstancy, dexterously circumvent the pointed rocks of Suspicion and battle with the wild waves of Fate, until it runs into the safe harbour of Happiness. Vol. IV, p. 12.

[xxiii] Many a man, indeed, may fall because he is too strong. For the diseased and withered oak stands firm against the storm, while the healthy one is laid low, because the tempest can seize upon its crown. Vol. I, p. 59.

[xxiv] She fell because she flowered too proudly and too strongly! The withered oak survives in the storm, while the healthy one is laid low crashing, because the tempest can seize its crown. Vol. II, p. 168.

[xxv] From now on you must endeavour to pay particular attention to all the phenomena that surround you. None is unimportant, all, even the seemingly most insignificant, contain something that is remarkable, if only we know how to perceive it. However, you must strive not only to perceive these phenomena, but also to learn from them. Ask yourself when faced by them, either: What does it betoken? and then the answer will enrich you with some useful lesson; or, if this is not possible, at least ask: What does it resemble? and then the discovery of the analogy will at least sharpen your mind. Vol. V, p. 160 f.

[xxvi] You know that I am now training myself to become a professional writer. I myself have begun a small Magazine of Ideas. Vol. V, p. 165.

[xxvii] Have patience—it won't always be like this and I long for a day, like a stag in the heat of noon for a stream into which it can plunge. But have patience! Patience? Can the heavens demand this from their creature when they have given it a heart full of yearning? Dissipation! Dissipation! Vol. V, p. 245.

[xxviii] First, sweet child, I must tell you that I am devoted to you in love, unutterably, eternally through all my senses. The stag which, anguished by the midday heat, tears up the earth with sharp antlers, does not long so voluptuously to plunge from the rock into the rushing forest stream, as I, now that you are mine, long to plunge into all your youthful charms. Vol. II, p. 308.

[xxix] How gently the moon shines through these tree-trunks! And how the brook far away in the forest with voluptuous splashing flows down from the rim of the high rocks! Thusnelda, come and quench this fire, lest I should, like a young stag, with head foremost, plunge into the waves. Vol. II, p. 439.

[xxx] A forceful and embracing soul is revealed by its powerful emotions. The ocean is shallow where the wind only casually ripples it, but it is deep where the wind towers up the waves. Vol. V, p. 183.

[xxxi] Just as the depths of the ocean always remain tranquil, however tempestuous the surface, so the expression of the figures of Greek sculpture, despite all passion, reveal a great and steadfast soul.

[xxxii] Man shall not endure every blow, and whom God seizes may, I think, fall, and also sigh, for equanimity is the virtue of athletes alone. We human beings surely do not fall for money or for show. But we should always be a worthy spectacle when we rise up again. Vol. I, p. 59.

[xxxiii] Hence sublimity is contained not in natural objects, but only in our minds, inasmuch as we are able to become aware of our superiority over nature within us and thus to nature . . . outside us.

[xxxiv] It is absolutely necessary to possess inward freedom of the mind in order to discover sublimity in terrible things and to derive pleasure from it. For they can only be sublime by virtue of the fact that they permit us to feel our own independence or freedom of mind.

[xxxv] Life never has anything more sublime to show than just this, that we can sublimely cast it away. Vol. V, p. 287.

[xxxvi] To produce and to sustain this freedom of mind within us is the happy task of comedy, just as tragedy is designed, by aesthetic means, to assist in the restoration of the freedom of our mind, when it has been violently upset by emotion.

[xxxvii] Equalization. Conciliatory rounding off, which is really demanded from all dramas and even from all poetic works. A reconcilement, a solution, is indispensable at the end, if a tragedy is to become a perfect work of art.

[xxxviii] What makes Kleist particularly odd, is his recipe for a dialogue. He imagines all his persons to be half deaf and stupid and so the dialogue comes into being by means of questions and repetitions.

[xxxix] Every great passion isolates. It hides away from its surroundings and seeks solitude, in order to dispute with itself, pity itself, exhort itself, take counsel with itself, denigrate itself, console itself, spend itself. The development of an interesting character is possible only through monologues.

[xl] Thus from the days of my earliest youth I have related all my general notions about poetry to musical tones. I believe that in the thorough bass may be found the most important information about poetry. Vol. V, p. 429.

[xli] At first there is an atmosphere, a musical one, which changes into colour; then I see figures, one or more, in some attitude or gesture, alone or in relation to others . . . Strangely, such an image or group is not as a rule the image of the catastrophe, but sometimes only a characteristic figure in some pathetic attitude; at once, however, a whole series is added to this image and I do not first experience the plot, the content of the fable, but from the situation which I had first seen, ever new plastic and mimic figures and groups coagulate, now forward towards the beginning, now towards the end, until I possess the whole play in all its scenes.

[xlii] My feeling at first does not possess a definite or clear object, which is formed later. A musical mood precedes and only afterwards does the poetic idea follow.

When I sit down to make a poem, the musical element hovers before my soul rather than a clear notion of its content, about which I am often hardly sure myself.

[xliii] One day the strange robing-scene of the last Act had come into Kleist's mind, simply as a scene, and since the situation attracted him, he had written it down as an isolated piece of fantasy. Only afterwards it occurred to him to weave it together with other threads of invention, perhaps also with a plot which he discovered by chance . . . And thus the whole tragedy gradually came to be woven around this scene.

[xliv] Kleist presents his story like a crime expert . . . In his works God remains hidden in the clouds and thus his idea of tragedy comes into

being. In his case it consists in the fact that human beings suffer and act without knowing for what reason and to what end.

[xlv] A work of art does not consist in that which is presented to our senses, but in the emotions engendered in us by the perception of sensual data. Vol. V, p. 342.

[xlvi] What always matters in art is form, and everything that has a shape is my business. Vol. V, p. 371.

[xlvii] Language, rhythm, euphony, etc., however attractive these things may be, inasmuch as they conceal the mind, are, nevertheless, in themselves nothing more than a real drawback, however natural and necessary; and, as far as they are concerned, art can only aim at making them disappear as far as possible. I exert myself to the best of my ability to give clarity to my expressions, significance to my verse, grace and vitality to the sounds of words; all this, however, in order that these things should not really be made manifest, but solely the idea which they envelop. The quality of all true form consists in this, that it reveals the mind directly and immediately, while a defective form, like a poor mirror, imprisons it and draws our attention to itself and to nothing else. Vol. IV, p. 149.

[xlviii] In a truly beautiful work of art the form should contribute everything, the content nothing.

[xlix] I add unarticulated sounds, expand conjunctions, occasionally make use of appositions where they are not really required, and avail myself of other devices which dilate speech, in order to gain enough time to manufacture my ideas in the workshop of reason. Vol. IV, p. 75.

[l] Furthermore I desire to follow my heart entirely wherever it leads me and take nothing into consideration except my own inward satisfaction . . . In short, I wish to be completely imbued with the idea that a work will necessarily belong to the whole of humanity, if it issues quite freely from the womb of the human mind. Vol. V, p. 430.

[li] When we really look into the matter, we find that in the last resort women are to blame for the whole decay of our stage and either they should not go to the theatre at all, or else special theatres should be built for them, separate from men. Their demands of propriety and morality destroy the whole nature of the drama. Vol. V, p. 359.

[lii] Goethe censures him for the Nordic acerbity of his hypochondria. It was, he said, impossible for a mature mind to enter with relish into the violence of the themes which he employed in his poetry. There was something hideous in nature, something frightening, to which poetry could neither apply itself, nor reconcile itself, however artistic the treatment.

[liii] The French say 'l'appétit vient en mangeant' and this empirical statement remains true if one parodies it and says 'l'idée vient en parlant.' Vol. IV, p. 74.

[liv] If therefore the expression of an idea is confused, it does not necessarily follow that the thought was confused. Vol. IV, p. 78.

[lv] It is not we who know, but there is to begin with a certain condition within us which knows. Vol. IV, p. 79.

[lvi] The error lies not in the heart, it lies in the intellect and the intellect alone can remove it. Vol. V, p. 209.

[lvii] It cannot be an evil spirit that presides over the world, it is merely one that has not been understood. Vol. V, p. 326.

[lviii] Penthesilea cannot be quite incomprehensible to those who love Käthchen. They belong together like the plus and the minus of Algebra, they are one and the same being conceived in opposite relationships. Vol. V, p. 380 f.

[lix] Every first movement, everything involuntary is beautiful, and everything becomes twisted and warped as soon as it comprehends itself. Alas, the intellect, the unhappy intellect! Vol. V, p. 328.

[lx] Grace is a kind of beauty which is not a gift of nature, but is produced by the subject itself. Grace is beauty of form under the influence of freedom, beauty of those manifestations which are determined by a person . . . Grace is always beauty of form set in motion by freedom, and movements which belong to nature only can never deserve this name.

[lxi] A voluntary movement to which is not added something involuntary that derives from the moral sense of a person, can never reveal grace, for which a condition of the mind is always the necessary cause.

[lxii] Grace is that which pleases rationally. It is formed by education and reflection and it can become natural in those who are fitted for it. It is far removed from constraint and deliberate wit, but diligence and industry are required to raise nature to the right degree of facility in every action in which grace can reveal itself in accordance with the talent of each person. Grace is active when the soul is in a state of harmony and at peace and it is obscured by a vehement fire and moments of inflamed passion.

[lxiii] It would be quite impossible for men even to vie with the puppet in this matter. Vol. IV, p. 138.

[lxiv] Because the force which lifts it into the air is greater than that which ties it to earth. Vol. IV, p. 137.

[lxv] I said that I well knew the havoc which consciousness caused in the natural grace of man. Vol. IV, p. 138.

[lxvi] We see that the more in the organic world the powers of reflection became dark and weak, the more grace emerged in it with ever greater radiance and power. Vol. IV, p. 141.

[lxvii] In this way grace reappears when knowledge has, as it were, passed through infinity, so that it is manifested in its purest form at the same time in that human shape which has an infinite consciousness and in that which has none, in the god and in the marionette. Thus, I said somewhat distractedly, we should have to partake again of the tree of knowledge, in order to fall back into the state of innocence. Certainly, he replied, that is the last chapter of the history of the world. Vol. IV, p. 141.

[lxviii] When even this dissatisfaction with fate disappears and is lost

in the intimation, or, better still, in the clear realization of a teleological relation between things, a sublime order, a benevolent will.

[lxix] A necessary product of naive thought is a naive expression in words as well as in movements and this is the most important component of grace.

[lxx] Man started with instinct and he shall end with instinct. Instinct is the genius in Paradise, before the era of self-isolation (self-knowledge).

[lxxi] The oldest relation of man with nature, the living harmony of the individual with the whole.

[lxxii] We do not often find that natural impulses are exposed to illusions or mistakes, such as, in a sense, is the case with the will.

[lxxiii] Never obey the dark urge, which always leads to vulgarity . . . Do what your first feeling tells you. Vol. V, p. 180.

[lxxiv] Brockes always said that the intellect was cold and the heart active and creative. Always he completely surrendered to his first impulse which he called his glimpse of feeling and I have never found that it disappointed him. Vol. V, p. 188.

[lxxv] It is true, my inmost being is contained in it. Vol. V, p. 358.

[lxxvi] If the spirits of Æschylus, Sophocles and Shakespeare collaborated to create a tragedy, it would be what Kleist's Death of Guiscard the Norman would have become, if the whole corresponded to the portion which he allowed me to hear. From that time onwards it was settled in my mind that Kleist was born to fill the great gap in our dramatic literature which, in my opinion at any rate, has not been filled even by Goethe and Schiller.

[lxxvii] Alonzo begs Fernando for peace. In vain. Vol. IV, p. 287.

[lxxviii] Fate is a juggler—storm of passion, rape of error, rage—makes fools of us. One might introduce a witch who really guided the hand of fate. At the end Ursula must enter as the guide of fate, in search of her child. Vol. IV, pp. 295, 303, 307.

[lxxix] Go away, old witch, go. You are a good juggler. I am satisfied with your trick. Go away. Vol. I, p. 158.

[lxxx] *Gertrude:* If I knew your present mood, I should be able to tell you much. *Sylvester:* It is a dreary day with much wind and much rain outside. An invisible power pulls everything with might in one direction, the dust, the clouds and the waves. *Gertrude:* Will you listen to me, Sylvester? *Sylvester:* That sail greatly occupies my mind. Do you see it? It tosses in great peril, its position is precarious, it cannot reach the shore. *Gertrude:* Listen to me, Sylvester, I have news for you about Jerome. *Sylvester:* It has got across. (He turns to her) I know everything. Vol. I, p. 119.

[lxxxi] Bring wine! Be merry! Wine! A joke that will kill us with laughter! Wine! The devil had blackened both their faces in their sleep. Now they know each other again. Villains! Wine! Let us have a toast! Vol. I, p. 158.

[lxxxii] *Santing:* The snake has a tough life. But I can swear to it. The sword sticks in her breast. *Rupert* (passes his hand across his face): Why did I do it, Santing? I cannot find any reason in my memory. *Santing:* Well, but it is Agnes. *Rupert:* Agnes, yes, indeed. She has done me wrong, much wrong. I know it well. What exactly was it? *Santing:* I don't know what you mean. The girl herself has not done you wrong. *Rupert:* No wrong? Santing! Why then should I have killed her? Tell me quickly, I beg you, how has she offended me—tell me with real malice— basilisk, don't look at me, speak, devil, speak—and if you do not know what to say, lie to me! Vol. I, p. 146 f.

[lxxxiii] Such is the curse of power that a decision that could be revoked quickly finds a helping hand that irrevocably chains the will to the deed. A master would not do one-tenth of evil, if he had to do it with his own hand. His mere thought breeds disaster and the meanest of his slaves has the advantage over him, since he is in a position to desire evil. Vol. I, p. 109.

[lxxxiv] It is distasteful to me. I will not admit that I have done it. Take it upon yourself. I'll throw you into the dungeon . . . When you are set free, the beautiful fief in the mountains will be yours. Vol. I, p. 110.

[lxxxv] That I should pacify him? My father? Dear Agnes, he carries us as the sea carries the ship. We have to follow his wave, we cannot appease it. No, I know a better way, for nothing will help, if the error that fools us does not come to light . . . Just another moment. One error can vanish as easily as another. I'll tell you what I shall do. It has always struck me that precisely the same little finger was missing from the two hands of my brother's corpse. I should have thought that every other part of the body would be more important for the murderer than just the little finger. If anything can be found out, this can be done only at the scene of the crime. I know where it is. I also know that some people live there. That is what I shall do—I shall go to them. Vol. I, p. 88 f.

[lxxxvi] Whatever the confession may be, my inmost feeling rises above it. Vol. I, p. 97.

[lxxxvii] For there is something that far transcends every piece of guess-work or knowledge, and that is the feeling of the goodness of another's soul. Vol. I, p. 82.

[lxxxviii] What is that? I am ashamed. By heaven, none is to blame for this but you, Gertrude. Suspicion is the black disease of the soul and for a diseased eye everything, even the innocent and pure, is clothed in the raiment of Hell. Insignificant, commonplace, quite ordinary things are cunningly woven, like scattered threads, into a picture that frightens us with its terrible shapes. Vol. I, p. 36 f.

[lxxxix] *Sylvester:* Your effort embarrasses me. Give me two moments and I shall put everything right and recuperate. *Gertrude:* At least take some drops from the little Tyrolese bottle which you yourself have always recommended as a remedy. *Sylvester:* No woman ever believes in her own

power and she puts more trust in a salve than in her soul. *Gertrude:* Believe me, it will fortify you. *Sylvester:* For that I only need my consciousness. (He rises.) What gratifies me is that the mind is greater than I thought. For when it momentarily absents itself, it only goes to its fountain scource, to God, and it returns with the strength of a hero. Vol. I, p. 56.

[xc] *Sylvius:* Whither do you lead me, boy? *Johann:* Into exile, old man, for I am folly. Console yourself, it is the right way. *Sylvius:* Alas, alas. In the forest walks blindness and its guide is madness. Take me home, boy, take me home. *Johann:* To happiness? It cannot be, old man. 'Tis locked on the inside. Come. We must go on. *Sylvius:* Must we? Then may heaven have mercy on us. Well, then, I follow you. Vol. I, p. 152 f.

[xci] O brothers, outcasts of fate, hand in hand we go into exile from Paradise whence the flaming sword of the Cherub drives us. Vol. IV, p. 293.

[xcii] *Jeronimus:* Let a priest unravel this confusion. I can't. *Sylvester:* Do I puzzle you? Well, console yourself. God puzzles me. Vol. I, p. 72.

[xciii] God of Justice! Speak clearly to men, so that they may know what to do. Vol. I, p. 151.

[xciv] The theme of Amphitryon is just as much the immaculate conception of the Virgin as the mystery of love itself, and thus the drama is descended directly from the noble and happy time, when the unity of all creeds, of all love and the great and inward community of all religions at last stood revealed.

[xcv] Contains nothing less than a Christian adaptation of the fable to adumbrate the overshadowing of Mary by the Holy Ghost.

[xcvi] A son will be born to you, whose name is Hercules. Vol. I, p. 311.

[xcvii] No, father Zeus, I am not satisfied and the tongue of my heart's desire grows. What you have done for Tyndarus, you will also do for Amphitryon. Grant him a son as great as the sons of Tyndarus. Vol. I, p. 311.

[xcviii] The real Amphitryon has to accept the fact that Zeus has done him the honour. In other ways the situation of Alkmene is embarrassing and that of Amphitryon at the end cruel.

[xcix] The Ancients in treating Amphitryon aimed at the confusion of the senses, the conflict between senses and convictions . . . The present poet, Kleist, aims, in the principal figures, at the confusion of feelings.

[c] How shall I find words, my Charis, to explain the inexplicable to you? Fleeing in terror to my chamber, not knowing whether I wake or dream when the insane assertion is hazarded that another man has appeared to me . . . and now, asking myself: did you err? For one of us is tricked by error: neither I nor he is capable of perfidy. And now that the ambiguous gibe streaks through my memory when the lover Amphitryon—did you hear it?—reviled the husband Amphitryon before me, now that terror and

I

-horror seize me and all my senses faithlessly desert me, I grasp, beloved Charis, the stone, the priceless, unique and dear pledge which is my truly infallible testimony. Vol. I, p. 253.

[ci] Is this hand my own? This breast my own? Does the image belong to me which is reflected by the mirror? He would be more a stranger to me than I myself. Take my eye from me, I shall hear him. Take my ear, I shall touch him. Take my touch from me and I shall still breathe him. Take eye and ear, touch and smell, all my senses, and grant me but my heart, then you will leave me the bell which I need, I shall still seek him out in a whole world. Vol. I, p. 254 f.

[cii] O my dearest Littegarde, the chamberlain cried, guard your senses against despair. Pile up the feeling which lives in your breast, like a rock. Hold on to it and do not yield, even if earth and heaven below and above you should perish. Let us think the more intelligible and rational thought of the two which confuse our senses and before you believe yourself guilty, rather believe that I was the victor in the duel which I fought for you!—Oh God, Lord of my life, he added and covered his face with his hands, guard my soul against confusion. Vol. III, p. 419.

[ciii] Not only am I denuded of all testimony, but this stone is a testimony against me. What can I in my confusion assert against it? . . . Tell me, am I certain that I really received from him the token which I have here? Vol. I, p. 257.

[civ] I could have taken him for his own picture, for a painting, true to life, but overdrawn by the hand of the artist to possess the contours of a god. He stood before me, I know not how, as in a dream, and I was seized by an ineffable feeling of my happiness, such as I have never known. Vol. I, p. 255 f.

[cv] To whom do you pray at his altar? Is it to him who resides above the clouds? Can your confined intellect really comprehend him? Can your feeling, at home in its nest, dare to move its wings for such a flight? Is it not always Amphitryon, the beloved, before whom you lie in the dust? Vol. I, p. 266 f.

[cvi] Very well, you shall be pleased with me. In the first hour of every morning no thought will henceforth dwell on you. Vol. I, p. 268.

[cvii] Accursed be the delusion that enticed me hither. Vol. I, p. 269.

[cviii] Alas, how unhappy I am, how you confuse me. Can one be guilty against one's will? Vol. I, p. 267.

[cix] If I were chosen for such a sacred office, may he who created me, dispose over me. Vol. I, p. 270.

[cx] *Jupiter:* If I should be this god for you? *Alkmene:* If you—What do I feel? If you were to be this god for me—I know not, shall I fall on my knees before you, shall I not? Are you that god, are you? *Jupiter:* Decide. I am Amphitryon. *Alkmene:* Amphitryon. *Jupiter:* For you, Amphitryon. But if, I ask, I should be this god for you, who loving you descended from Olympus for you, how then would you be able to contain

yourself? *Alkmene:* If, dearest, you were this god for me—then indeed I should not know where Amphitryon might be for me. I should follow you wherever you go, even, like Eurydice, to Orcus. *Jupiter:* If you did not know where Amphitryon might be. But what if Amphitryon should now reappear? *Alkmene:* If Amphitryon—alas, you torture me. How can Amphitryon appear before me, if I hold Amphitryon in my arms? *Jupiter:* And yet you could well hold the god in your arms in the belief that it is Amphitryon. Why should your feeling surprise you? If I, the god, here embraced you and Amphitryon now appeared before you, how would your heart then decide? *Alkmene:* If you, the god, here embraced me and now Amphitryon appeared before me, well, then I should be so sad and wish that he could be the god and that you could continue to be my Amphitryon, as you now are. Vol I, p. 270 ff.

[cxi] Can any one understand it? Does it make sense? Can one grasp it? Vol. I, p. 233.

[cxii] I used to hear about miracles, about unnatural apparitions which stray from another world into this, but to-day the thread from beyond is fastened to my honour and strangles it. Vol. I, p. 243.

[cxiii] There is some deception here, that is clear, but my senses cannot yet grasp the cursed web. Vol. I, p. 247.

[cxiv] If she can recognize him as her husband, I no longer ask who I am. I shall acclaim him Amphitryon. Vol. I, p. 304.

[cxv] Now I swear an oath on the altar and instantly die a sevenfold death in the imperturbable belief that for her he is Amphitryon. Vol. I, p. 308.

[cxvi] You monster! More revolting to me than that which battens in morasses. Vol. I, p. 306.

[cxvii] Not until now do I see what a delusion confounded me. I needed the bright radiance of the sun to distinguish such a base frame of vulgar knaves from the glorious structure of these royal limbs, the bullock from the stag! Cursed be the senses which succumb to so palpable a deception! Cursed the breast which gives forth such dissonant tones! Cursed the soul that is not worth so much as to remember its own beloved! Vol. I, p. 307.

[cxviii] We know a little play, bearing the same name, by the author of 'Käthchen von Heilbronn'. This play and the following story originated on the same occasion in Bern in the year 1802. Heinrich von Kleist and Ludwig Wieland, the son of the poet, were friends of the present author, in whose room hung a copper engraving entitled La cruche cassée. The expressive drawing gave much pleasure and led to many interpretations of its content. Jokingly the three friends pledged themselves that each of them would elaborate his own view in writing. Ludwig Wieland promised a satire, Heinrich von Kleist planned his comedy and the author of the following tale that which is here given.

[cxix] The following comedy is probably based on an historical event

about which I have, however, not been able to obtain much information.
I took the opportunity of writing the play from a copper engraving which
I saw in Switzerland several years ago. The picture showed first a judge
who gravely sat on his seat of judgment; in front of him stood an old
woman who held a broken jug in her hand and appeared to demonstrate
the injury that had been done to it. The accused, a young peasant lad,
against whom the judge stormed as though he had been convicted, still
defended himself, but only feebly; a girl who had probably given evidence
in the case (for who knows on what occasion the misdeed had taken
place) stood between her mother and her fiancé and played with her apron;
nobody who has given false evidence could stand there more dejectedly;
and the notary, who had perhaps a moment before looked at the girl,
now looked at the judge distrustfully with a sidelong glance, like Creon,
on a similar occasion, at Œdipus when the question was asked who had
killed Laius. Underneath was written: The Broken Jug. The original, if
I am not mistaken, was by a Dutch master. Vol. IV, p. 318.

[cxx] She said: 'Go, my sweet child. Mars calls you. You will crown
the son of Peleus with garlands. Become a mother proud and happy as I
am,' and gently pressed my hand and died. Vol. II, p. 119.

[cxxi] It is not fitting that a daughter of Mars should seek her adversary.
She shall choose whom the god allows to appear before her in battle.
Vol. II, p. 120.

[cxxii] I thus bethought myself: if all the great moments of history
were repeated for me, if the whole gathering of heroes, whom the noble
songs celebrate, descended for me from the stars, none shall I find to
garland with roses excelling him whom my mother chose for me, the dear,
savage, sweet, terrible, the vanquisher of Hector! O son of Peleus! You
were my everlasting thought when I was awake, my everlasting dream!
The whole world lay spread out before me like an embroidery canvas;
into every mesh, large and spacious, one of your deeds was worked and
into my heart, white and pure like silk, I burned each one with flaming
colours. Vol. II, p. 121 f.

[cxxiii] Instantly, son of Peleus, I guessed the source whence that feeling
rushed into my breast. The god of love had overtaken me. Vol. II, p. 122.

[cxxiv] *The Captain:* Every artifice of speech was exhausted to lead her
back to Themsicyra. But she seemed deaf to the voice of reason. Her
youthful heart, it is said, has been struck by the most poisonous dart of
Amor. *The High Priestess* (to the Captain): The queen, you say? Impossible, my friend! Struck by the dart of Amor—when? And where?
The leader of the diamond belt? Mars' daughter, she who has no breast,
the target of those poisoned winged arrows? *The Captain:* Thus says at
least the voice of the people, and Meroe has just confided it to me. *The High
Priestess:* It is dreadful . . . Oh, she treads the steep path down to Orcus!
And not to the adversary when she encounters him will she fall, but to the
enemy in her own bosom. Vol. II, pp. 67 ff.

[cxxv] *Prothoe:* Go away, you maidens, go away. Return to your native pastures. The queen and I, we shall remain here. *The High Priestess:* Unhappy woman, you confirm her wish? *Meroe:* Is there no escape for her? *The High Priestess:* None, since nothing restrains her from outside, no fate, nothing but her foolish heart. *Prothoe:* That is her fate. Bonds of iron seem unbreakable to you, do they not? Behold, she could break those and still not be able to break the feeling which you deride. She alone knows the power that holds sway within her and every feeling heart remains a mystery. Vol. II, pp. 77 f.

[cxxvi] [See no. xxiv].

[cxxvii] That evening before the most important day of my life, I went for a walk in Würzburg. When the sun was setting it seemed to me that my happiness was going down, too. I shuddered at the thought that perhaps I had to depart from everything that was dear to me. Absorbed in my meditations, I returned to the town through the vaulted gateway. Why, I thought, does the vault not collapse, since it has no support? It remains standing, I replied, because all the stones are about to fall at the same time—and I derived an inexpressibly refreshing solace from this thought. Vol. V, p. 160.

[cxxviii] Come, my queen. Raise yourself. You will not fall now. Often when everything goes under in man, this supports him, as the vault remains standing because each of its blocks is about to collapse. Vol. IV, p. 338.

[cxxix] So you are raising yourself up? Well, my queen, then do it like a giant. Do not fall, even if the whole of Orcus weighed you down! Stand, stand firm, as the vault stands, because each of its blocks is about to collapse! Proffer your head, like a keystone, to the bolts from the gods and cry: Strike! And let yourself be split asunder down to your feet! but in yourself waver no more as long as a breath of mortar and stone holds together in your breast. Vol. II, p. 81.

[cxxx] True, I can wing a swallow in such a way that it can be cured. I entice a deer into the park with arrows. But the art of the marksman is treacherous, and when it comes to the master shot into the heart of fortune, then cunning gods guide our hand. Vol. II, p. 160.

[cxxxi] [See no. cxxi].

[cxxxii] They derive their race from Mars . . . Some, however, assert in particular that they are the daughters of Mars and Harmonia, a naiad . . . Others, again, believe that only some of them are the daughters of the afore-mentioned god.

[cxxxiii] Through his priestess the god shows us a splendid and chaste nation which shall appear in his place as his representative. Vol. II, p. 116.

[cxxxiv] Hasten at once, Arsinoe, to her presence and tell her in the name of my goddess that Mars has presented himself to his brides and that I exhort her on penalty of Diana's anger now to lead the god home garlanded and without delay to begin his sacred feast of the roses in the temple. Vol. II, p. 66.

[cxxxv] Behold, twenty times and three I had experienced the happy feast of the roses and always from afar, where the temple rises above the grove of oak trees, heard the joyful acclamations, when Ares, at the death of Otrere, my mother, chose me for his bride. For the princesses of my royal house never of their own free will mingle in the feast of the blossoming maidens. When the god desires them, he calls upon them in a worthy manner through the mouth of the great High Priestess. Just as my mother lay pale and dying in my arms, the solemn ordination of Mars was revealed to me in the palace, and I was called upon to depart for Troy, thence to lead him back garlanded. Vol. II, pp. 118 f.

[cxxxvi] Whenever after yearly calculations the queen desires to make good to the state the number of those whom death has snatched away, she calls the flower of maidenhood from the corners of her realm to Themiscyra and in the temple of Artemis prays that the blessing of the chaste fructification of Mars descend into their young wombs. Vol. II, p. 116.

[cxxxvii] To please the shade of Otrere rather than Mars, the great god, who called me thither. Vol. II, p. 121.

[cxxxviii] Thus I must have felt if instantly he had thundered down from Olympus with his white chargers, Mars himself, the god of war, to greet his bride. Vol. II, p. 122.

[cxxxix] Suddenly she lays aside the reins. We see her, like one overcome by giddiness, quickly pressing her forehead, encircled by a flood of locks, against her two small hands. All the maidens swarm around her, confounded by this strange spectacle. Vol. II, p. 32.

[cxl] Why? Wherefore? What has happened? What have I said? Have I — What is it that I have — ? Vol. II, p. 50.

[cxli] *Penthesilea* (who during this time has fixedly gazed at the sun): That I might with wings wide spread and rustling, divide the air. *Prothoe:* What? *Meroe:* What did she say? *Prothoe:* What do you behold, my queen? *Meroe:* On what is fixed — ? *Prothoe:* Beloved, speak. *Penthesilea:* Too high, I know, too high—he plays in circles of flame eternally removed around my ever loving bosom.

Penthesilea: One thing more, my friends, and you yourselves will admit that I should be mad if I did not try out the whole field of possibilities. *Prothoe:* (angered) Well, then, I should prefer it that we were annihilated at once, for we cannot be saved any more. *Penthesilea:* (startled) What is it? What is wrong? What have I done to her? O maidens, speak! *High Priestess:* You intend — ? *Meroe:* You still desire, in this place — ? *Penthesilea:* Nothing, nothing, nothing at all that need enrage her. I wish to pile Ida upon Ossa, only to place myself calmly on the top. *High Priestess:* Pile Ida — ? *Meroe:* Pile on Ossa — ? *Prothoe:* (turning) Protect her, all you gods. *High Priestess:* She is lost. *Meroe:* (with diffidence) That is the work of giants, my queen. *Penthesilea:* What of it, what of it? Why should I be inferior to them? *Meroe:* Why should you be — ? *Prothoe:* Heavens! *High Priestess:* But assuming? *Meroe:* Assuming now you accomplish this work — ? *Prothoe:* Assuming that, what would you — ? *Penthesilea:* Stupid woman! I should pull him down to me by his flaming gold hair. *Prothoe:* Whom? *Penthesilea:* Helios, when he flies past me above my head. (The princesses look at each other, speechless in horror). Vol. II, pp. 80, 82 f.

[cxlii] Kneels down, showing all the signs of madness. Vol. II, p. 134.

[cxliii] *High Priestess:* Do you hear him, my queen, how enraged he is against you? *Penthesilea:* With all his thunder I call him down upon me. Vol. II, p. 133.

[cxliv] Nay, rather than that I should fail to accomplish what has so splendidly, so nobly begun for me, rather than that I should fail utterly to seize the crown that rustles on my brow, rather than fail to do what I promised to do, to lead the daughters of Mars exultingly to the pinnacle of fortune, rather may its pinnacle come crashing down on me and on them: now curse the heart that knows not how to curb itself. Vol. II, p. 52.

[cxlv] Is it my fault that I must with arms contend in the field of battle for his feelings? What is it that I want when I draw my sword on him? Do I want to hurl him down to Orcus? Eternal gods, I only want, only want to draw him down to my bosom. Vol. II, pp. 72 f.

[cxlvi] A curse upon this shameful triumph! . . . Is there a law, I ask, in such a war, which can set free the prisoner who has surrendered, from the bonds of his victor? Vol. II, p. 128.

[cxlvii] This breast of mine, does it only move him when his sharp lance has shattered it? What I whispered to him, has it struck his ear only with the melody of speech? Vol. II, p. 132.

[cxlviii] Since the strength of the bow could never be controlled by feeble women, impeded by their full breasts, as easily as by men. Vol. II, p. 113.

[cxlix] After this deed silence reigned, son of Peleus. Nothing but the fluttering of the bow was heard, which fell from the hands of the High Priestess, rigid and pale as a corpse. It fell, the great, the golden bow of the realm and clattered three times upon the marble steps amid the thundering peal of bells and silent as death it lay down at her feet. Vol. II, p. 114.

[cl] *The first Amazon:* The bow falls down from her hand.
The second Amazon: Behold how it staggers.
The fourth Amazon: Clatters and sways and falls.
The second Amazon: And once more on the ground it jerks.
The third Amazon: And dies, just as it was born for Tanais.
Vol. II, p. 152.

[cli] And—in confidence, a word that none should hear. The ashes of Tanais, scatter them to the winds. Vol. II, p. 166.

[clii] For now I descend into my bosom, as into a shaft, and dig out a feeling, cold as iron ore, that will annihilate me. This ore I purify in the glow of distress until it becomes as hard as steel. Then I soak it through and through with poison, the hot, corroding poison of remorse, carry it

to the eternal anvil of hope and sharpen and point it until it is a dagger. And to this dagger I now proffer my breast. Thus, thus, thus, thus, and again. Now it is well. (Falls and dies.) Vol. II, p. 167.

[cliii] The judgment of other people has hitherto dominated my work too much. Käthchen von Heilbronn particularly is full of traces of this. To begin with, it was an excellent invention and only my intention of making it suitable for the stage led me to make mistakes over which I could now weep. Vol. V, p. 430.

[cliv] When Kleist had written 'Käthchen von Heilbronn' and had communicated it to Tieck, they had frequent discussions and disputes about it and Tieck, among other things, expressed his opinion about a remarkable scene which in a sense diverted the whole piece into the realm of the fairy tale or of magic. Kleist misunderstood this view and took it to be a criticism, destroyed the scene, without Tieck's knowledge, and when he later missed it in the printed text, he could not stop voicing his regret, since this scene gave a much better motivation of the caricatured ugliness of Kunigunde and put it in a better light. According to this scene Käthchen in the fourth Act was walking on the rock and below in the water a sprite appeared to her and called to her with words and song. Käthchen was on the point of jumping down and was only saved by a companion. Before that she had espied Kunigunde bathing in her ugliness and was beside herself with anxiety to save the knight from this monster.

[clv] O you, how shall I call you, Käthchen! Why cannot I call you my own? Kate, maid, Kate! Why cannot I call you my own? Why do you leave your golden frames, you pictures of my ancestors in arms, who populate my armoury and collect around me in a restless gathering, shaking your venerable locks? No, no, no! I do not desire her for a wife although I love her. I shall join your proud ranks; that has been decided upon, even before you came here. Vol. II, p. 212.

[clvi] So be it. It shall not disturb the feeling which is kindled here in my bosom.
I demand that nothing shall contradict the feeling that is kindled in my bosom. Vol. II, pp. 229, 239.

[clvii] What God has joined, it is said, man shall not sunder. Vol. II, p. 307.

[clviii] Hail to you, Marbod, my magnanimous friend! And if Germany will hear my voice, hail to her great overlord and king! Vol. II, p. 451.

[clix] A curse on him, if he has done that to me! For a moment he has embezzled my heart, made me a traitor to Germany's great cause. Why else did he set fire to Thuiskon? I will not love the arrogant brood from Hell! As long as they hold out in Germany, my office is hate and my virtue revenge. Vol. II, 406 f.

[clx] My pretty Thuschen! I acclaim you a heroine. How nobly and magnificently you have kept your word! Vol. II, p. 449.

[clxi] But every falsehood is but a pledge of faith to the fatherland.

[clxii] *Hohenzollern:* In the devil's name, speak! Cannot you guess the face? Which lady do you mean? *Prince Friedrich:* No matter, no matter, the name escaped me when I woke up. Vol. III, p. 30.

[clxiii] He commands that you shall not reveal a word to the Prince when he wakes up, about the prank which he permitted himself to play with him. Vol. III, p. 26.

[clxiv] Now upon your globe, Immensity, from whom the breeze to-day lifts the veil like a sail, roll towards me! Already, Fortune, you have touched my locks. Already in passing you have thrown down a pledge to me from your horn of plenty. To-day I shall seek you, child of the gods, fugitive one, I shall seize you in the field of battle and pour out the whole of your blessing at my feet, even if with sevenfold chains of iron you are fastened to the Swedish victory chariot. Vol. III, p. 44.

[clxv] *Prince Friedrich:* There is something I wanted to tell you, Heinrich (He leads the count a little to the front): What was the order concerning me that Dörfling gave yesterday at the meeting? *Hohenzollern:* You were distracted, I saw that. *Prince Ferdinand:* Distracted, divided. I don't know what was the matter. Dictations confuse me. *Hohenzollern:* Fortunately not much for you this time. Truchss and Hennings who lead the infantry have been chosen to attack the enemy and you have to halt here in the valley with the cavalry, ready to strike, until the word of command to attack is sent to you. *Prince Friedrich:* (after a pause in which he was lost in thought) A curious episode! Vol. III, p. 48.

[clxvi] I had sent Major Hennings, as well you know, to remove the Swedish bridge-head covering Wrangel's rear. If you had not disobeyed the order, Hennings would have succeeded with this stroke. In two hours' time he would have set the bridges on fire, taken position on the Rhyn, and Wrangel would have been utterly destroyed in the ditches and the marshes. Vol. III, p. 111.

[clxvii] It is for bunglers, not for you, to seek the highest laurels of fate. Vol. III, p. 111.

[clxviii] Rome was not built in a day. Vol. III, p. 112.

[clxix] By order, Kottwitz! Do you gallop so slowly? Have you never yet received an order from your heart? Vol. III, p. 52.

[clxx] The base, short-sighted policy of state, which, for the sake of one instance, when feeling proved fatal, forgets ten others in the course of events, when feeling alone could save. Vol. III, p. 113.

[clxxi] Do you believe that fortune will always, as she did recently, reward disobedience with a crown? I do not desire the victory, which, a child of chance, is an illegitimate offspring. I desire to uphold the law, the mother of my crown, which will produce for me a progeny of victories. Vol. III, p. 112.

[clxxii] *Golz:* Have you found the marshal Dörfling? *Kottwitz:* (advancing) By Satan, no! What does his Excellency think? Am I an arrow,

a bird, a thought, that he can race me through the whole battlefield? Vol. III, p. 46.

[clxxiii] The Swedes were faltering on the left wing and on the right wing they brought up support. If he had waited for your order, they would have gained a footing once more in the ravines and never would you have gained the victory. Vol. III, p. 111.

[clxxiv] You strange old gentleman, I cannot get it straight with you. Vol. III, p. 113.

[clxxv] The Elector is lost in thought. Vol. III, p. 117.

[clxxvi] Fool that you are, idiot! If you had not called me into the garden, I should not, on an impulse of curiosity, have played a harmless game with your dreamer. Hence I maintain with equal right that it is you who are responsible for his neglect. The Delphic wisdom of my officers! Vol. III, p. 118.

[clxxvii] Enough, my Prince. I am sure my words fell weightily into your breast. Vol. III, p. 118.

[clxxviii] The Elector has done what duty demands. Now he will also listen to his heart. Vol. III, p. 73.

[clxxix] The tribunal was compelled to pass the sentence of death. Such is the law, according to which it judges. But rather than allow the verdict to be carried out, rather than expose this heart of mine which loyally loves him, to the bullets, when a piece of cloth is waved, rather, surely, he will pierce his own breast and shed his own blood in drops into the dust. Vol. III, p. 75.

[clxxx] The laws of war, I know, must prevail, but so also must sweet feelings. Vol. III, p. 88.

[clxxxi] By my oath, I swear to you. How can I oppose the opinion of such a warrior? As you know well, in my inmost heart I have the greatest respect for his feelings. If he can believe that the verdict is unjust, I'll cancel the edict. He will be free. Vol. III, p. 90.

[clxxxii] My Prinz von Homburg, when I arrested you because of the attack which you accomplished too early, I believed that I did no less than my duty. I reckoned on your own approval. If you believe that an injustice has been done to you, I beg you to tell me in a few words and instantly I shall return your sword to you. Vol. III, p. 97.

[clxxxiii] That he did me wrong, which is the condition asked of me, this I cannot write to him. Vol. III, p. 100.

[clxxxiv] Guilt, serious guilt, weighs upon my breast, as I well recognize. If he can only pardon me when I quarrel with him about that, then I will have none of his mercy. Vol. III p. 102.

[clxxxv] You yourself I ask. Can I suppress the verdict which the tribunal has pronounced? Vol. III, p. 87.

[clxxxvi] How could he call me to this table of judges who, heartless, like owls, ever sing me a song of death and bullets, if he does not wish to

enter their circle with a serene word of royal command like a god? Vol. III, p. 74.

[clxxxvii] I wish to glorify, by a voluntary death, the sacred laws of war which in the face of the army, I have violated. Vol. III, p. 120.

[clxxxviii] Let him do what pleases him; it behoves me here to act as I should. Vol. III, p. 101.

[clxxxix] Mere power, however terrible and absolute, cannot lend majesty. Power impresses only the sensual in man, majesty must deprive the mind of its freedom. A human being who can sign my death warrant, does not for that reason possess majesty over me, as long as I am myself what I should be. His advantage over me vanishes as soon as I desire it. But he who represents the pure will in his person, before him I shall, even in future worlds, if that should be possible, bow in reverence.

[cxc] True unselfishness is revealed in the ability never to be affronted by the selfishness of others, just as much as, and even more than, in the ability always to anticipate it. Therefore never accuse another of this failing. If he does not understand your voluntary sacrifice, remain silent and do not chide, and when he demands a sacrifice from you, do it, as long as it is possible, and he may thank you or not, be silent once more and do not chide. Vol. V, p. 193.

[cxci] She did not, I believe, understand the art of sacrificing herself, of totally perishing for the object of one's love, which is the greatest boon one can think of on earth, indeed the boon of which heaven must consist, if it is true that we are to be happy and contented there. Vol. V, p. 433.

[cxcii] My one and all, my wife, my marriage, the baptism of my children, my tragedy, my fame. Vol. V. p. 403.

[cxciii] Add to this the fact that I have found a friend whose soul mounts like a young eagle, such as I have never before found in my life, who understands that my sorrow is a higher, firmly rooted and incurable one and therefore, although she possesses enough means to make me happy here, wishes to die with me, who grants me the unheard-of delight of allowing herself, for this purpose, to be lifted as easily from a situation filled with contentment for her, as a violet from a meadow . . . and you will appreciate that my only exultant care can be to find a chasm deep enough to throw myself into it with her.

Oh, I assure you I am quite happy. In the morning and in the evening I kneel down and pray to God, which I have never been able to do until now; now I can thank Him for my life, the most tortured that any man has had, since He rewarded me by the most glorious and sensual of deaths . . . The resolve which dawned in her soul, to die with me, drew me, I cannot tell you with what inexpressible and irresistible force, to her bosom. Do you remember that many a time I asked you whether you would die with me? But you always said no. Vol. V, 435 f.

ADDENDUM

Translation of passage quoted on p. 82, beginning 'Und sag' ihr . . . '
And tell her that her great ancestor Mars has granted the wish of the
people and that I, the great High Priestess of Diana, now exhort her to
return home instantly for the celebration of the Feast of the Roses.
Vol. IV, p. 336.

CHRONOLOGICAL TABLE OF KLEIST'S LIFE AND WORKS

October 18, 1777	Born in Frankfurt on the Oder.
June 1788	Death of father.
June 1792	Enters the Prussian Army.
February 1793	Death of mother.
March 1799	*Aufsatz, den sichern Weg des Glücks zu finden.*
April 1799	Resigns commission. Enters Frankfurt University.
1800	Engagement to Wilhelmine von Zenge.
August 1800	Journey to Würzburg.
August 1800–1801	*Ideenmagazin.* Study of Kant's philosophy.
1801	Visit to Paris. Beginnings of *Robert Guiskard* (published 1808) and of *Die Familie Schroffenstein* (published 1803).
1801–2	Visit to Switzerland. Beginnings of *Der Zerbrochene Krug* (completed 1808, published 1811).
1804	Lives in Berlin.
1805	Occupies civil service post in Königsberg.
1806	*Über die allmähliche Verfertigung der Gedanken beim Reden. Amphitryon* (published 1807). Beginnings of *Penthesilea* (completed and published 1808).
1807	Arrested by the French and sent to Fort Joux near Besançon.
July 1807	Lives in Dresden. Friendship with Adam Müller, and attendance at G. H. Schubert's lectures. Beginnings of *Das Käthchen von Heilbronn* (published 1810).
1808–1809	*Phöbus, Die Hermannsschlacht* (published 1821).
February 1810	Lives in Berlin. *Prinz Friedrich von Homburg* (published 1821).
1810–1811	*Berliner Abendblätter.* Publication of *Über das Marionettentheater* and *Brief eines Dichters.*
November 21, 1811	Commits suicide on the shore of the Wannsee near Berlin.

SELECT BIBLIOGRAPHY

R. Ayrault: *Heinrich von Kleist*, 1934.
 La Légende de H. von Kleist: Un poète devant la critique, 1934.
A. Béguin: *L'Ame Romantique et le Rêve*, 1937.
F. v. Biedermann: *Heinrich von Kleists Gespräche*, 1912.
J. C. Blankenagel: *The Attitude of H. v. Kleist toward the Problems of Life*, 1917.
 The Dramas of Heinrich von Kleist, A Bibliographical and Critical Study, 1931.
P. Böckmann: *Kleists Aufsatz über das Marionettentheater*, Euphorion, 1927.
F. Braig: *Heinrich von Kleist*, 1925.
F. Bruns: *Die Motivierung aus dem Unbewussten bei Heinrich von Kleist*, Studies in German Literature in Honor of A. R. Hohlfeld, 1925, pp. 47 pass.
E. v. Bülow: *Heinrich von Kleists Leben und Briefe*, 1848.
Edmund Burke: *A Philosophical Inquiry on the Origin of our Ideas of the Sublime and Beautiful*.
E. Cassirer: *Heinrich von Kleist und die kantische Philosophie* in Idee und Gestalt, 1921.
J. Collin: *Heinrich von Kleist, der Dichter des Todes*, Euphorion, 1926.
M. Corssen: *Kleist und Shakespeare*, 1930.
Benedetto Croce: *Kleist* in Poesia e Non Poesia, 1923.
D. G. Dyer: *Amphitryon: Plautus, Molière and Kleist*, German Life and Letters, 1952.
E. Edelmann: *Das sittliche Gesetz in Kleists Prinz von Homburg*, Zeitschrift für Deutschkunde, 1920.
Barker Fairley: *Heinrich von Kleist*, Modern Philology, XIV, pp. 321 ff.
G. Fricke: *Gefühl und Schicksal bei Heinrich von Kleist*, 1929.
 Kleists Prinz von Homburg, Versuch einer Interpretation, Germanisch-Romanische Monatsschrift, 1951–1952.
 Penthesilea in Das Deutsche Drama ed. B. v. Wiese, 1958.
A. Fries: *Stilistische und vergleichende Forschungen zu Heinrich von Kleist*, Berliner Beiträge zur germanischen und romanischen Philologie, Germanische Abteilung, 1906.
I. Appelbaum Graham: *The Broken Pitcher*, Modern Language Quarterly, 1955.
F. Gundolf: *Heinrich von Kleist*, 1922.
Abbé Guyon: *Histoire des Amazons*, 1740.
H. Herrmann: *Studien zu Heinrich von Kleist*, Zeitschrift für Ästhetik, 1924.
W. Herzog: *Heinrich von Kleist*, 1911.
P. Hoffmann: *Der zerbrochene Krug, ein Lustspiel geboren aus dem Geist der Tragödie*, 1941.

T. Käiser: *Vergleich der verschiedenen Fassungen von Kleists Dramen, Sprache und Dichtung,* 1944.

H. Klein: *Die antiken Amazonensagen in der deutschen Literatur,* 1919.

P. Kluckhohn: *Die deutsche Romantik,* 1924.

F. Koch: *Heinrich von Kleist, Bewusstsein und Wirklichkeit,* 1958.

I. Kohrs: *Das Wesen des Tragischen im Drama Heinrich von Kleists,* 1951.

M. Kommerell: *Die Sprache und das Unaussprechliche, Eine Betrachtung über Heinrich von Kleist in Geist und Buchstabe der Dichtung,* 1944.

J. T. Krumpelmann: *Kleist's Krug and Shakespeare's Measure for Measure, Germanic Review,* 1951.

Shakespeare's Falstaff Dramas and Kleist's Zerbrochene Krug, Modern Language Quarterly, 1951.

E. Kühnemann: *Kleist und Kant, Jahrbuch der Kleistgesellschaft,* 1922.

C. Lugowski: *Wirklichkeit und Dichtung,* 1936.

Thomas Mann: *Kleists Amphitryon in Adel des Geistes,* 1945.

R. March: *Heinrich von Kleist,* 1954.

H. Meyer-Benfey: *Das Drama Heinrich von Kleists,* 1911–1913.

G. Minde-Pouet: *Heinrich von Kleist, seine Sprache und sein Stil,* 1897.

W. Müller-Seidel: *Prinz Friedrich von Homburg in Das Deutsche Drama* ed. B. v. Wiese, 1958.

W. Muschg: *Kleist,* 1923.

L. Muth: *Kleist und Kant, Versuch einer neuen Interpretation,* 1954.

J. Niejahr: *Heinrich von Kleists Penthesilea, Heinrich von Kleists Prinz Friedrich von Homburg, Vierteljahrsschrift für Literaturgeschichte,* 1893.

J. Petersen: *Heinrich von Kleist und Torquato Tasso, Zeitschrift für deutschen Unterricht,* Vol. XXXI.

Kleists dramatische Kunst, Jahrbuch der Kleistgesellschaft, 1921.

M. Prigge-Kruhoeffer: *Heinrich von Kleist, Religiosität und Charakter, Jahrbuch der Kleistgesellschaft,* 1923–1924.

S. Rahmer: *Das Kleist-Problem,* 1903.

K. v. Reinhardstoettner: *Plautus, Spätere Bearbeitungen plautinischer Lustspiele,* 1886.

F. Röbbeling: *Kleists Käthchen von Heilbronn. Bausteine zur Geschichte der neueren deutschen Literatur,* 1913.

H. Roetteken: *Heinrich von Kleist,* 1907.

Friedrich Schiller: *Über Anmut und Würde, Briefe über die ästhetische Erziehung des Menschen.*

A. Schlagdenhauffen: *L'Univers existentiel de Kleist dans Le Prince de Hombourg,* 1953.

M. Schoch: *Kleist und Sophokles,* 1952.

H. J. Schrimpf: *Der zerbrochene Krug in Das Deutsche Drama* ed. B. v. Wiese, 1958.

G. H. Schubert: *Ansichten von der Nachtseite der Naturwissenschaft,* 1808.

K. Schultze-Jahde: *Zur Interpretation von Kleists Schauspiel Prinz Friedrich von Homburg, Jahrbuch der Kleistgesellschaft,* 1927–1928.

B. Schulze: *Das Bild als Leitmotiv in den Dramen Kleists und anderer Dichter,* *Zeitschrift für den deutschen Unterricht,* Vol. XXIV.

F. Servaes: *Heinrich von Kleist,* 1902.

D. F. S. Scott: *Heinrich von Kleist's Kant Crisis. Modern Language Review,* Vol. XLII, pp. 474 ff.

W. Silz: *Heinrich von Kleist's Conception of the Tragic,* 1923.
   The Kinship of Heinrich von Kleist and Otto Ludwig, Publications of the Modern Language Association, 1925.
   Otto Ludwig and the Process of Poetic Creation, ibid., 1945.

G. Stefansky: *Ein neuer Weg zu Heinrich von Kleist, Euphorion,* 1921.

J. Sully: *Pessimism,* 1891.

R. Tymms: *Alteration of Personality in Kleist and Werner, Modern Language Review,* Vol. XXXVII.

R. Unger: *Herder Novalis Kleist,* 1922.

O. Walzel: *Leitmotiv in Dichtungen, Zeitschrift für Bücherfreunde,* Vol. VIII.

R. Weissenfels: *Vergleichende Studien zu Heinrich von Kleist, Zeitschrift für vergleichende Literaturwissenschaft,* 1887.

R. F. Wilkie: *A new Source for Kleist's Der zerbrochene Krug, Germanic Review,* 1948.

P. Witkop: *H. v. Kleist,* 1922.

H. M. Wolff: *Heinrich von Kleist, Die Geschichte seines Schaffens,* 1954.

S. Wukadinović: *Über Kleists Käthchen von Heilbronn, Euphorion, Ergänzungs-heft,* 1895.

G. Zeissig: *Heinrich von Kleists Dramensprache, Zeitschrift für Deutschkunde,* 1929.

S. Zweig: *Der Kampf mit dem Dämon,* 1925.

INDEX